A Lion Dead
to the Lord

A Lion Dead to the Lord

Inspired by The Holy Spirit

Recorded by Frederick A. Prince

ISBN: 1494915057

Library of Congress Number: 2015917528

Printed in the United States of America

Published by Frederick A. Prince

Email: fprince101@gmail.com

Table of Contents

"The gospel says you are more sinful and flawed than you ever dared believe, but more accepted and loved than you ever dared hope." —Timothy Keller

Foreword

*"C*rucify, crucify Him!"*

This is what the chief priest, the leaders and the people kept shouting to Pilate.

Pilate asked, "Why, what evil has he done?" (Lk 23:22)

When St. Stephen, in the Acts of the Apostles, gave his defense to the High Priest, they were so consumed with anger; they immediately dragged Stephen out and stoned him to death. (Acts 7: 58)

The Jews already had stones in their hands for the penalty of death as they dragged the adulteress woman in front of Jesus. (Jn 8: 3)

They drove Jesus out of the town and led Him to a cliff which they intended throw Him over. (Lk 4: 29)

The Jews at that time were not afraid of executing the death penalty instantly if they felt the circumstances called for it.

So, why was Jesus crucified?

After He was judged guilty of blasphemy why not stone Him right then and there?

This has been a question that has consumed my thinking for the past three years, after the Holy Spirit first planted the idea for this book in my mind.

More than once I have heard a priest or minister ask the question, "Did Jesus have to be crucified?"

If we ask the question, "Did Jesus have to be crucified in order that we might be justified to God the Father?"

I believe the answer is NO.

Jesus, the Human Christ, Son of God, the Creator of the universe; Jesus could have pricked His finger and we would have been justified.

I can't comprehend what the full meaning of "Son of God" means.

Go outside tonight and look up at the stars. At His Father's request, Christ, the Devine Son, created the Heavens.

The question then has to be asked: Why did God the Father choose Crucifixion as the method for Jesus to die?

Over the past three years, as I worked on this book, I realized the answer was that God the Father, Son and Holy Spirit wanted to teach us how to live a life only known to the prophets before Jesus, and totally unknown to ordinary man, before the death of Jesus.

My journey started one night during a book group meeting, hosted by Monsignor Henchal. After the meeting, my whole life opened up to a new Jesus, one I had never known, and one I love even more.

The Book Group

For the past 20 years, St. Bartholomew's church of Cape Elizabeth, Maine, has had a book study group. This past year, the group was hosted by our pastor, Msgr. Michael Henchal. The book we were discussing for me was a hard read.

One night, Msgr. Henchal decided to demonstrate how the Gospel of Mark was copied and expanded upon by Matthew and then given more detail by Luke. The part of the Bible he used to illustrate his point was Jesus being buried.

What was interesting to me was, if Msgr. Henchal had used any other Biblical event, or had started reading the Gospel story before Joseph of Arimathea was mentioned, **A Lion Dead to the Lord** wouldn't have been written.

The Holy Spirit at work in my life!

What Msgr. Henchal read:

Mark:
When evening had come, and since it was the day of Preparation—that is, the day before the Sabbath—Joseph of Arimathea, a respected member of the council, who was also himself waiting expectantly for the kingdom of God, went boldly to Pilate and asked for the body of Jesus.

*Then Joseph bought a linen cloth, and taking down the body, wrapped it in the linen cloth **and laid it in a tomb that has been hewn out of the rock. He then rolled a stone against the door of the tomb.***
(Emphasis mine, Mk. 15:42-43:46)

Matthew:
There came a rich man from Arimathea, named Joseph, who was also a disciple of Jesus. He went to Pilate and asked for the body of Jesus. Then Pilate ordered it to be given to him.

*So Joseph took the body and wrapped it in a clean linen cloth **and laid it in his own new tomb,** which he had hewn in the rock. He then rolled a great stone to the door of the tomb and went away. Mary Magdalene and the other Mary were there, sitting opposite the tomb.*
(Emphasis mine Mt. 27:57-61)

Luke:
Now there was a good and righteous man named Joseph, who, though a member of the council, had not agreed to their plan and action. He came from the Jewish town of Arimathea, and he was waiting expectantly for the kingdom of God. This man went to Pilate and asked for the body of Jesus.

*Then he took it down, wrapped it in a linen cloth, and laid it in a rock-hewn tomb **where no one had ever been laid.***
(Emphasis mine Lk 23: 50-53)

According to the book, **The Historical Jesus** written by John Dominic Crossan, not the book we were reading in Msgr. Henchal's group, Jewish tombs at the time of Jesus were carved into rock and had shelves to hold more than one body. An entire family could be buried in one tomb.

Matthew said, and *laid it in his own new tomb.* I always felt the tomb was for Joseph of Arimathea only.

The Historical Jesus also explained Luke's statement, *where no one had ever been laid.* The tomb was a family tomb, and no one in the family had been buried in the tomb before the burial of Jesus.

As Msgr. Henchal read Mark, Mathew, and Luke, I noticed, Holy Spirit, the name Joseph of Arimathea was also mentioned in each of the three gospels.

Msgr. Henchal wanted to demonstrate Mark being the basis of Matthew, and then Luke, and the details of Jesus' burial being expanded by each.

I was drawn to Joseph of Arimathea.

When I arrived back home, I decided to look at John's Gospel to see how John handled the burial of Jesus and see if John also mentioned Joseph of Arimathea.

John:
After these things, Joseph of Arimathea, who was a disciple of Jesus, though a secret one because of his fear of the Jews, asked Pilate to let him take away the body of Jesus. Pilate gave him permission; so he came and removed his body. Nicodemus, who had at first come to Jesus by night, also came, bringing a mixture of myrrh and aloes, weighing about a hundred pounds.

Now there was a garden in the place where he was crucified, and in the garden there was a new tomb in which no one had ever been laid. And so, because it was the Jewish day of Preparation, and the tomb was nearby, they laid Jesus there.
(Jn 19:38-42)

As I read the four Gospels, I noticed that each Apostle gave new information about Joseph of Arimathea.

Joseph was respected (Mark), rich (Matthew), good and righteous and had not agreed on the plan (Luke), and was a secret disciple (John).

Not only is Joseph's name mentioned four times, but we are given a clear picture of the type of man he was. In fact, we know more about Joseph of Arimathea from his Biblical description than we do from the descriptions of the majority of the twelve Apostles.

This, to me, is fascinating because this is one of the few times in the New Testament where a piece of information, Joseph of Arimathea, is mentioned by all four Evangelists.

Consider how many major events aren't mentioned in all four Gospels.

The establishment of the Eucharist at the Last Supper is mentioned in Matthew, Mark and Luke.

John talks about the washing of feet—service.

The Our Father is mentioned in Matthew and Luke.

The details of the Birth of Jesus are mentioned in Matthew and Luke.

The Centurion said at the death of Jesus that Jesus was the Son of God, in Mark and Matthew.

Luke said Jesus was innocent.

You might think the above would be mentioned in all four gospels, but they're not.

What we discussed that night was the burial process.

As I drove home I was urged by the Holy Spirit to look up Arimathea.

What did this word mean?

I'm 73, and I love to read. But in my 73 years, I don't recall ever looking up a word to see what it meant.

I have an iPad and don't use its dictionary to look up any words.

Yes, you guessed it, I am intellectually lazy. I say this because when the thought to look up Arimathea came to me I knew the Holy Spirit, was working within me.

I went to the web site www.netministeries.org
Clicked on: Biblical Words Pronunciation Guide – A
Clicked on: Arimathea
Below Arimathea
Clicked on: Hitchcock's Bible Names Directory
Clicked on – A
Clicked on: Arimathea

This is what came up: "A Lion Dead to the Lord!"

A Lion Dead to the Lord!

I repeated the phrase "A Lion Dead to the Lord" to myself a few times; and my mind started to reel at the implications.

A Lion Dead to the Lord!

My first thought: Jesus, a Lion?

I had always thought of Jesus as the Lamb of God, the Second Person of the Holy Trinity, Emmanuel, the First Fruit, the Light of the World, the Son of Man, just to mention a few titles. I never once considered Jesus to be a Lion of God. This, for me, changed everything.

A Lion Dead to the Lord!

All four Gospels mention Joseph of Arimathea and provide details about him. We believe the Bible is the inspired word of God. God the Father wants us to know His Son was a Lion during His entire lifetime and His Crucifixion.

Jesus fought and defeated Satan, by living as a Lion of God.

How Jesus fought has even greater implications.

To expand on this, let's look at the **Old Testament**, the **New Testament, the Battle,** and how **Jesus' Death Applies to Us**.

The life, death and resurrection of Jesus enabled man to be justified to God the Father.

But...

Was Jesus' death on the Cross?

Passive?

Lamb only: as I believed for most of my life?

Active?

Lion only: as I am just starting to learn?

Both?

Through His death on the Cross, Jesus was walking the walk and teaching us how we are to live our lives and therefore, I believe should be viewed as active.

The Old Testament

The Old Testament

The Old Testament points to Jesus, and His Cross.

Some of the Old Testament readings that point directly to the death of Jesus:

Around the year 740 BC, Isaiah, started to prophesy about the death of Jesus, and how Jesus would act during His death.

Other prophets told about the Messiah, but Isaiah was specific about the manner in which the Messiah, Jesus, would die... "Like a lamb led to slaughter."

I gave my back to those who struck me,
and my cheeks to those who pulled out the beard;
I did not hide my face
from insult and spitting.
The Lord God helps me;
therefore I have not been disgraced;
therefore I have set my face like flint.
(Is 50: 6-7)

He was oppressed, and he was afflicted,
yet he did not open his mouth;
like a lamb that is led to the slaughter,
and like a sheep that before its shearers is silent,
so he did not open his mouth.
(Emphasis mine Is 53:7)

While hanging on the Cross, Jesus cried with a loud voice, "Eli,
Eli, lema sabachthani?" That is, "My God, my God, why have
you forsaken me?"
(Mt 27:46)

For years I couldn't figure what Jesus was saying.

It sounds like Jesus is crying out for help.

He couldn't!

Why?

Isaiah prophesied He wouldn't. Jesus would die *like a sheep*
that before its shearers is silent!

Jesus lived in the Love, Joy and Peace of the Holy Spirit while
He was being crucified.

I finally realized Jesus was saying the first words of the 22nd
Psalm. It is not a cry for help, but Jesus declaring victory over
Satan from His Cross.

It is only when we read the end of the 22nd Psalm that we see
that the psalmist predicted the Victory that Jesus would win
from His Cross.

If I were to say for example, "Our Father who art in Heaven,"
you would know this was the start of the Lord's Prayer, given to
us by Jesus in the Gospel of Saint Matthew (Mt 6: 9-13).

When Satan heard the start of 22nd Psalm while Jesus was hanging on the cross, he must have shuddered, for the ending of this psalm tells of the end of Satan, and the victory won by Jesus.

The last lines of this Psalm are:

To him, indeed, shall all who sleep in the earth bow down;
before him shall bow all who go down to the dust,
and I shall live for him.
Posterity will serve him;
future generations will be told about the Lord,
and proclaim his deliverance to a people yet unborn,
saying that he has done it.
(Ps. 22:29-31)

There it is: *All who sleep will bow down, Proclaim his deliverance to a people yet unborn,* Jesus will win, Jesus did win. We are delivered from the grasp of Satan by the death and resurrection of Jesus.

You don't bow to a loser!

Jesus won!

Love always wins!

Satan also knew the 22nd Psalm was before the 23rd Psalm, The Lord Is my Shepherd.

Do you think the two psalms are side by side by accident?

I don't!

Jesus referred to himself as the Good Shepherd.

In May of 2012, I volunteered to be a lector at Saint Bartholomew's Church. Finally in November of 2012, I was given my first readings.

As I studied the readings, I was stunned. The first reading revealed that Satan was driven by envy, and through envy Satan would try to defeat Jesus.

I must admit, having six months go by before I was called to do my first readings was very frustrating.

I now know why God wanted me to wait.

The Holy Spirit wanted these readings to leap out at me for this book.

As you read these next two passages from the book of Wisdom, know that the words were written 50 years before the Birth of Jesus.

God did not make death,
and he does not delight in the death of the living.
For he created all things so that they might exist;
the generative forces of the world are wholesome,
and there is no destructive poison in them,
and the dominion of Hades is not on earth.
For righteousness is immortal.
for God created us for incorruption,
and made us in the image of his own eternity,
but through the devil's envy death entered the world,
and those who belong to his company experience it.
(Emphasis mine NABRE Wis 1:13-15; 2:23-24)

Envy, this was the driving force of Satan!

Envy, Jesus always did the will of His Father!

Satan was thrown out of Heaven because he rebelled against doing the will of God the Father.

Adam and Eve ate the apple to be equal to God.

If I am equal to God, guess what?

I don't need God!

Envy employs physical and emotional pain to gain an advantage. Envy would be the energy used by Satan to try and break Jesus.

Pilate knew that. *"It was out of envy that they handed Him over."* (Mt 27:18)

Envy is destructive!

Love, Joy and Peace are constructive.

A month later, I was lector for the second time; the first reading was again from the book of Wisdom.

The wicked say:
Let us beset the just one, because he is obnoxious to us;
he sets himself against our doings,
reproaches us for transgressions of the law
and charges us with violations of our training.
Let us see whether his words be true;
let us find out what will happen to him.
For if the just one be the son of God, God will
defend him
and deliver him from the hand of his foes.
With revilement and torture let us put the just one to the test
that we may have proof of his gentleness
and try his patience.
Let us condemn him to a shameful death;
for according to his own words, God will take care of him.
(NABRE Wis 2:12, 17-20)

In the Gospel of Matthew, chapter 23, we see that Jesus was obnoxious to the Pharisees, scribes and Jewish leaders (Mt 23:13-15). He did call them hypocrites not once but many times in the gospels, as predicted in the book of Wisdom 50 years before His birth.

He did set Himself against their doings (Mt 23:29-36).

He did reproach them for transgressions of the law (Mt 23:23-24).

And:

He did charge them with violations of their training (Mt 23:16-22).

God "telegraphed" in the book of Wisdom why Jesus would suffer the type of death He did.

What really leaped out at me was:

*With revilement and torture let us put the just one to the test
that we may have proof of his **gentleness**
and try his **patience**.
Let us condemn him to a shameful death;
for according to his own words, God will take care of him.*
(Emphasis mine, NABRE Wis 2:19-20)

Gentleness and Patience are two of the nine Fruit of the Holy Spirit. If you don't know the nine Fruit of the Holy Spirit, and I sadly believe many don't, this statement will mean very little to you.

Jesus is the First Fruit (1 Cor 15:23)! As long as Jesus lives during His crucifixion, in the Fruit of The Holy Spirit, Love, Joy and Peace, Jesus wins!

The Cross!

No question.

Satan now had over 600 years since Isaiah, and 50 years after the writing of the book of Wisdom, to design a form of death that would employ maximum pain to break Jesus from being the Sacrificial Lamb, and dying in the Fruit of The Holy Spirit.

Satan would employ envy.

Envy of the Love that the Father has for the Son, and envy of the love that the Son has for the Father, that Love being the Holy Spirit.

Jesus would live in the Fruit of the Holy Spirit during His Crucifixion and teach us from His Cross; Patience, Kindness, Generosity, Faithfulness, Gentleness and Self-Control.

But you ask, did God the Father take care of Jesus? For it said, *"God will take care of Him."*

Yes, He did!

Here am I, Lord; I come to do your will.
Sacrifice or oblation you wished not,
but ears open to obedience you gave me.
Burnt offerings or sin-offerings you sought not;
then said I, "Behold I come."
"In the written scroll it is prescribed for me,
To do your will, O my God, is my delight,
and your law is within my heart!"
I announced your justice in the vast assembly;
I did not restrain my lips, as you, O LORD, know.
May all who seek you
exult and be glad in you,
And may those who love your salvation
say ever, "The LORD be glorified."
(NABRE Ps 40:7-8A, 8B-9, 10, 17)

Once again I was lector, and this passage was one of the readings.

The words "to do your will is my delight," "exult" and "be glad" leaped out at me.

Yes, God the Father took care of Jesus which I will discuss later in the book!

In English I can say I love my wife, job, meal or just about anything else.

To say God the Father, Son and Holy Spirit loves us, I don't think conveys the Love they have for us and what They—Father, Son and Holy Spirit—would and did do to demonstrate Their Love.

At Mass one Sunday, Msgr. Henchal said God's love was an OUTRAGEOUS LOVE.

Yes, it was Outrageous Love and still is!

All the "worldly" evidence would indicate that Jesus was in intense pain.

But!

Jesus lived in the Holy Spirit—the "Spirit World," a world of Outrageous Love, and in the "Spirit World," as we will discuss, things are very different.

Setup for the Battle

When humans go into battle, we take great efforts to make sure the enemy doesn't know what our intentions are.

The Americans and British established a phony division in England during World War II to get the Germans to believe the invasion was going to take place at Calais and not Normandy.

When the Japanese bombed Pearl Harbor, it was a sneak attack.

God does not fight the way man does.

God told Satan what would happen and what the result would be.

Remember, God does love Satan. This might sound odd, but God loves not part of the time, or some of creation, but all the time for all creation.

*In Catholicism, the Catechism of the Catholic Church speaks of
"the fall of the angels" not in spatial terms but as a radical and
irrevocable rejection of God and his reign by some angels who,
though created as good beings, freely chose evil, their sin being unforgivable because of the irrevocable character of their
choice, not because of any defect in the infinite divine mercy.*
(Wikipedia, Fallen Angel)

An Angel never goes half way. They are either with God, doing
His will, or against God. If they turn away from God, they can't
come back.

Why?

Angels have full knowledge of God!

We don't! Jesus acknowledged this from the Cross *"Father, forgive them; for they do not know what they are doing."*
(Lk 23:34)

When the Angels rebelled against God, because of their full
knowledge of God, their sin was irreversible.

No riding the fence!

The battle that would take place during Jesus's death was a
battle in every sense of the word. This battle would establish
whether the world would be run under Envy, the power of Satan, or Outrageous Love, a Spiritual World, an entirely different
way of life.

Arimathea is another great example of the setup for the upcoming battle.

Consider hundreds of years before the birth of Jesus, a Jewish
town was given the name Arimathea, and the definition of Arimathea:

A Lion Dead to the Lord.

Was this by chance?

I don't think so.

What also are the odds that a prominent man from Arimathea, a secret follower of Jesus, would be the person to go to Pontius Pilate and ask for the body of Jesus?

No, this is the hand of God working, and the setup for the upcoming battle is beautiful.

Reading the Old Testament starts to give us a glimpse of the upcoming battle.

You might ask why did God telegraph what would happen to Jesus in the Old Testament?

God living in the present, I AM, while predicting the future, demonstrates clearly that God is God.

The New Testament

The New Testament

I am going to very briefly trace the life of Jesus in the Gospel of Luke.

After each quote you determine was Jesus acting as a Lion or a Lamb?

There were also many lepers in Israel in the time of the prophet Elisha, and none of them was cleansed except Naaman the Syrian." When they heard this, all in the synagogue were filled with rage. They got up, drove him out of the town, and led him to the brow of the hill on which their town was built, so that they might hurl him off the cliff. But he passed through the midst of them and went on his way.
(Lk 4:27-30)

Is this the statement of a Lion or Lamb?

Then he said to them, "The Son of Man is lord of the Sabbath."
(Lk 6:5)

Would a Lion or Lamb make the outrageous claim that He was Lord of the Sabbath?

"If you then, who are evil, know how to give good gifts to your children, how much more will the heavenly Father give the Holy Spirit to those who ask him!"
(Lk 11:13)

Would a Lamb call the people He was talking to evil?

In the three above examples, Jesus attacked the conventional thinking of the Jews.

These are not the words of a lamb!

Now, when I read the gospels, I think of Jesus as also being a Lion, exactly what God the Father had intended.

Interesting!

How did I miss this for 72 years?

It's not just me. When people asked me if we, the Holy Spirit and I, were working on another book, which I had indicated on the back cover of **A Journey with The Holy Spirit**, I replied yes.

I then told them the title of this book and asked; who is the Lion I am writing about?

Only one person came up with the correct answer. That person was my brother Roger. He knew the answer because he had read the **Chronicles of Narnia** by C.S. Lewis, which I hadn't read, to his daughter Kaitlin. In that book, Jesus is portrayed as a Lion.

Sad!

We know more about the battles of Bunker Hill, Gettysburg, and Normandy, than the greatest battle in the history of man, Jesus fighting Satan during His entire lifetime and during His last hours on earth.

Jesus Fully Human

After the Last Supper, Jesus and His disciples went to the Mount of Olives.

Question: Why didn't the Jews arrest Jesus after he left the room where the Last Supper was being held?

Judas knew where Jesus ate.

Judas was there!

Why wait until Jesus goes to the Mount of Olives? It was nighttime; grab Him as they are walking through the narrow streets of Jerusalem.

Luke said Judas *accepted their offer and sought a favorable opportunity to hand him over to them in the **absence of a crowd.***
(Emphasis mine NABRE Lk 22:6)

Interesting, they crucified Jesus, outside the city, but in front of all the people of Jerusalem.

God instilled the fear of condemnation from the crowds into the leaders and Judas, so God the Father could show His, Jesus' humanity, and teach us to do His, the Father's will, as Jesus did from His Cross.

Jesus knew He would be scourged and crucified. He had predicted this earlier in His ministry. (Lk 18: 31)

No sane human would approach being crucified without asking if they really had to go through with it.

Jesus asked just that question.

Then he withdrew from them about a stone's throw, knelt down, and prayed, **"Father, if you are willing, remove this cup from me**; *yet, not my will but yours be done." Then an angel from heaven appeared to him and gave him strength. In his anguish he prayed more earnestly, and his sweat became like great drops of blood falling down on the ground.*
(Emphasis mine Lk 22:42-44)

Satan's ears picked up at these first few words.

Then:

Jesus said, *"Not my will but yours be done."*

The Lion of God is victorious!

Jesus is fully human.

If God the Father would allow Jesus to skip the Cross, that would be okay.

But!

Jesus was a human who would only do the will of His Father, no matter the cost—even death on a cross.

These words, doing the will of God the Father, are easy to type.

Why does it seem so hard to live?

I once walked into a meeting and the topic of discussion was what they couldn't or wouldn't give up, if asked to do so by God the Father.

Isn't this the same question Jesus asked at the Mount of Olives?

I'm not being critical. I have stated that I have the same problem and wrote about my experiences of learning to do the Father's will in **A Journey with the Holy Spirit**.

For some reason, and that reason was my listening to Satan, I felt that God the Father would ask of me that which I couldn't do, or even worse, ask me to do something that would make my life less joyful.

The Cross!

My cross!

As I related in **A Journey with the Holy Spirit**, God told me to get rid of the group medical insurance I had sold and serviced for over five years, because of abortion on demand. Our company would lose 40 percent of its income by my doing His will.

I rebelled at the thought of losing all that income, and refused to do the Father's will. The Holy Spirit withdrew from me, and I experienced life void of the Holy Spirit.

For three days I stubbornly refused to change, and paid dearly for it, the third day was Sunday and after mass I talk to Msgr. Henchal about my problem. He saw the fear in my eyes. I know this because years later we talked about this episode, and he vividly remembered all the details.

He said drop the group health insurance!

I thought "Wrong Priest."

Monday I grudgingly did as God asked, and a few years later thanked God because the renewal process and trying to get un-paid claims paid was very stressful.

I stupidly felt it was a test to see if I would give up the money I earned.

No!

God the Father wanted me to reduce my stress so I could grow closer to the Holy Spirit.

If Jesus had been abducted as He walked through the streets of Jerusalem, we wouldn't have seen Jesus fully human. I am sure more than one person would have said since He wasn't fully human, He didn't really die.

In fact, as we will discuss in the chapter titled "Jesus Dies on the Cross," the Muslims believe Jesus didn't die on the Cross or anywhere else. The Muslims believe Jesus was a prophet, but not fully human.

Only humans die!

Not being human would mean Jesus never really experienced life as you and I do.

In the Christians' eyes, if Jesus was not fully human, He is a fraud!

How could Jesus claim he lived as we live if He never died?

He couldn't!

Earlier in my life I hoped God the Father somehow gave Jesus Heavenly Novocain to eliminate the pain Jesus would experience during His last hours on earth.

After much thought, I realized that if God the Father gave Heavenly Novocain only to Jesus, and no one else, Jesus couldn't stand in front of us and claim He lived and understood all we went through, because He hadn't.

What I now realize is God the Father did take care of Jesus and will take care of us.

Why Death on the Cross?

In the Acts of the Apostles, St. Stephen, the first Christian martyr, was stoned to death.

Stephen was accused of blaspheming and was immediately executed.

The story of the martyrdom of St. Stephen:

"Look," he said, "I see the heavens opened and the Son of Man standing at the right hand of God!" But they covered their ears, and with a loud shout all rushed together against him. Then they dragged him out of the city and began to stone him; and the witnesses laid their coats at the feet of a young man named Saul.
(Ac 7:56-58)

They took Stephen out and stoned him!

Jesus before the High Priest:

"From now on you will see the Son of Man seated at the right hand of Power and coming on the clouds of heaven." Then the high priest tore his clothes and said, "He has blasphemed! Why do we still need witnesses? You have now heard his blasphemy. What is your verdict?" They answered, "He deserves death." Then they spat in his face and struck him; and some slapped him, saying, "Prophesy to us, you Messiah! Who is it that struck you?"
(Mt 26: 64-68)

With Jesus, the High Priest said, "He has blasphemed." Why didn't they drag Him out and stone Him?

Both Jesus and Stephen related Jesus as being at the right side of God, a position of power. One they crucified, the other they stoned.

Odd?

Why, then, death on a Cross?

A few reasons that come to my mind:

If Jesus had been stoned to death, we'd miss the entire Outrageous Love story, battle and crushing defeat of Satan that unfolds over the last hours of Jesus life on earth.

We miss Jesus walking the walk!

We miss the life lessons that will be taught from the Cross.

We miss the Lion of God fighting evil as evil has to be fought in order to obtain victory—with Outrageous Love!

Jesus' death had to be so outrageous that all of humanity would know of it. And when someone first learns how Jesus died, they would have a hard time with the idea that God would die in the manner that Jesus did, on a Cross.

The death of Jesus forces man to view God—Father, Son and Holy Spirit—like no other god man had ever worshipped before.

I can't think of any god or prophet before Jesus who submitted themselves to a cruel death, and forgave their executioners while they were dying.

Only Jesus!

I remember the movie **The 300 Spartans**, when the Persian god king came ashore carried on a throne by a hundred-plus slaves.

The slaves put the throne on the ground and then ran out in front of the throne and knelt down to create a human walkway for the god king, so the god king's feet wouldn't touch the soil.

Before Jesus, human life had little or no value.

Jesus lived in the "Spirit World," a life in total opposition to the "world" at that time and in opposition to those living in the "world" today.

The Cross, once a symbol of a brutal death, is now a symbol of Love, Joy and Peace.

Only God could do this!

From the Cross we have been taught to forgive those who have transgressed against us:

Then Jesus said, "Father, forgive them; for they do not know what they are doing."
(Lk 23:34)

Every Thursday I volunteer at the Cumberland County Jail in a Bible study program. I tell the men they have to forgive everyone who has screwed them over. They ask why.

Love, Joy and Peace will not co-exist with hate.

If Jesus is a teacher, and He is, then we should learn from His example when He forgave those who Crucified Him. (Lk 23:34)

Notice I didn't say, "Do as he told us."

His Cross gave Him the perfect opportunity to walk the walk.

Paul wrote in Colossians 3:13: *"Forgive each other; just as the Lord has forgiven you."* Paul didn't mention the Cross in this statement but that is where Jesus forgave us from, His Cross.

Now we have to choose.

Forgive and grow in Love, Joy and Peace.

Or:

Hang onto the hate, and live a life of anger.

I, for one, lived in anger in my younger years.

An example of my anger:

I had to learn to forgive the people who caused me to be fired from Morse Payson & Noyes. This took time. As I started forgiving them, I started to discover Peace. This all took place at a very dark moment in our life financially.

I would love to say I learned my lesson about anger, but that is not true. This is a continuous battle for me, the big difference now is I want to live in the "Spirit World" and will fight to stay there.

I never want go back to my old life of living in the "world"!

What I also realized was until I knew and experienced the Peace of the Holy Spirit; I had no way of learning how to grow in the Peace of the Holy Spirit.

Before I found the Holy Spirit, I experienced peace when I climbed mountains or walked in the woods.

I didn't know the Holy Spirit, so I couldn't link my peace to the Holy Spirit. I therefore couldn't figure out how to grow in the peace I was experiencing, while I was hiking.

Being fired was one of my personal crosses, and I will note it was a strange time to discover Peace, or was it, did God have to wait until I hit bottom before I would truly seek Him out?

Sadly, yes He did!

Not God's fault – Mine!

The really interesting thing is I realized my firing was the best thing that could have happen to me. Bottom line, I wasn't a manager!

I slowly learned that the Peace of the Holy Spirit will not co-exist with hate.

My only choice, then, was to Forgive and grow in the "Spirit World," and leave the "world" behind.

The prisoners have told me they can see a change in their lives as they learn and grow in the Fruit of the Holy Spirit.

They are now experiencing a new life, life in the Holy Spirit, and embrace the change that forgiving others has brought into their lives.

From the Cross Jesus welcomes the first person into Heaven.

Who?

The man crucified on His right.

He replied, "Truly I tell you, today you will be with me in Para-
dise."
(Lk 23:43)

A criminal who admits his guilt, repents and asks to be remembered, he, a criminal, is going to Heaven.

The criminal, the first Christian, Baptized by desire, by his own
admission is defiantly a sinner, and most importantly he is sorry for his sin.

Luke 13: 19 tells us the Prophets are in Heaven, which you
would expect, they were prophets, but a criminal, the first to
be saved after the death of Jesus:

This is an outrageous act of Love!

We started the book quoting Timothy Keller.:

"The gospel says you are more sinful and flawed than you ever
dared believe, but more accepted and loved than you ever
dared hope."

The criminal on the right proves this statement to be absolutely
true.

If St. Stephan had been the first to go to Heaven, I for one,
looking over my life would feel I had little chance of being with
Jesus in Heaven.

Now I truly believe St. Paul when Paul say's *we are justified by*
faith (Rm 5:1). The Criminal on the right believed Jesus when
Jesus said the criminal would be with Jesus in Paradise.

He is in Paradise!

The Battle

Betrayal

What better way to start a battle than to have one closest to Jesus betray Him? To be effective, the betrayer has to have the element of surprise.

In my job as a vice president of Morse Payson & Noyes, I was totally taken by surprise when those whom I managed let the company ownership know I wasn't a great manager.

I was the victim of a corporate coup.

I felt a knife had been driven into my back.

I was fired from the job that, quite frankly, had become my god, and had been defeated by those whom I managed.

It hurt!

That's an understatement!

The betrayal of Jesus starts when Judas Iscariot seeks out the chief priests.

What happened?

Then Satan entered into Judas called Iscariot, who was one of the; he went away and conferred with the chief priests and officers of the temple police about how he might betray him to them. They were greatly pleased and agreed to give him money. (Lk: 22 3-5)

The key words are Satan entered into Judas.

What did Satan say to Judas?

I believe Judas wanted Jesus to use His powers, which Judas had observed, over the three years they were together, to throw out the Romans and restore Israel to its former glory.

If Judas could accomplish this then Judas would also have great power, because he was the one who forced Jesus' hand.

Judas never understood what Jesus' mission on earth was.

Before the Holy Spirit was infused into their souls, the remaining 11 suffered from the same confusion.

Consider for a moment: Jesus has risen from the dead, appeared before the 11, and showed them His hands, feet and side, confirming to Thomas that He was alive. Yet after all these events, Peter said, "I am going fishing." (Jn 21:3)

"I am going fishing"?

Peter, you saw:
The tomb was empty (Lk 24:12)
You fed the 5,000 (Lk 9:13-17)
Lazarus raised from the dead (Jn 11:44)
Six stone water jars changed into wine at the wedding at Cana

(Jn 2:2-11)
10 lepers who were healed (Lk 17:11-19)

"I am going fishing"?

By saying "I am going fishing," Peter wanted to return to that with which he was most comfortable with. Fishing!

Peter and the Apostles were not ready to follow in Jesus' foot-steps—i.e., doing the will of God the Father.

It wasn't until the Holy Spirit was infused into their Souls that they were ready to do God's will.

Why did Judas hang himself?

Judas never believed he could be forgiven.

Jesus said all sins would be forgiven, except sins against the Holy Spirit (Mt 12: 31-32). Judas heard the words, but didn't believe.

For betrayal to work, it has to be a surprise. At the Last Supper, before He was betrayed, Jesus told His disciples that He would be betrayed.

After saying this, Jesus was troubled in spirit, and declared, "Very truly, I tell you, one of you will betray me." The disciples looked at one another; uncertain of whom he was speaking. One of his disciples—the one whom Jesus loved—was reclining next to him; Simon Peter therefore motioned to him to ask Jesus of whom he was speaking. So while reclining next to Jesus, he asked him, "Lord, who is it?" Jesus answered, "It is the one to whom I give this piece of bread when I have dipped it in the dish." So when he had dipped the piece of bread, he gave it to Judas son of Simon Iscariot. After he received the piece of bread Satan entered into him. Jesus said to him, "Do quickly what you are going to do." (Jn 13:21-27)

Betrayed, yes—surprised, no!

Jesus wins!

The battle has started.

The Agony in the Garden

I n writing this book, my eyes were finally opened to what took place during the Agony in the Garden.

The night before the execution, his disciples reported seeing Jesus in "agony" on the Mount of Olives. Not only did he not sleep all night, but he seems to have been sweating profusely. So great was the stress that tiny blood vessels were rupturing in his sweat glands and emitting as great red drops that fell to the ground (see Luke 22:44). This symptom of severe stress is called hematohidrosis. (christiananswers.net)

In the **New American Bible Revised Edition,** the title of the chapter of Jesus going to the Mount of Olives to pray to His Father is:

The Agony in the Garden
This title is used in Mt 26, Mk 14, Lk 22.

John in His Gospel is silent about Jesus asking His Father to take this cup from Him.

This is another great example of an important piece of information, The Agony in the Garden, not being in all four Gospels.

This, to me, was interesting because one might think His Scourging and Crucifixion would be titled The Agony of His Scourging and the Agony of His Crucifixion.

There're not!

When I started this book, the Holy Spirit led me to use the Gospel of Luke.

Why?

One reason: **The Agony in the Garden.**

"Father, if you are willing, take this cup away from me; still, not my will but yours be done." And to strengthen him an angel from heaven appeared to him. He was in such agony and he prayed so fervently that his sweat became like drops of blood falling on the ground.
(Lk 22:42-44)

Notice: *"He prayed so* fervently *that His sweat became like drops of blood falling on the ground."*

The other Gospel writers did not say His sweat became like drops of blood, only Luke, a Greek doctor.

I noted in **A Journey with the Holy Spirit** that the Holy Spirit withdrew slightly from Jesus so Jesus could experience the "world" without the Holy Spirit.

I've said slightly because of the Outrageous Love that Jesus has for His Father is so great that just a slight pullback by the Holy Spirit would cause His sweat to become like drops of blood.

When I mentioned that the Holy Spirit pulled back from me in 2004, when I said I wouldn't drop the group health insurance that the Spirit had told me to drop, my world came crashing down upon me.

The Holy Spirit withdrew, and for the next three days I experienced a stress I had never felt before, nor ever want to experience again.

It was absolutely the worst experience I have ever had. Far worse than any medical pain I have ever experienced.

I've had a few painful experiences in my lifetime—a dry socket, kidney stones, pancreatic attack, and three broken fingers, to mention just four. The pain from these paled in comparison to the Holy Spirit withdrawing from me.

I knew the cause, my not willing to do the will of God the Father, and I knew how to rectify the situation.

Do His will!

Drop the group!

Three days later, on Monday, I finally relented and started dropping the group health insurance, and at the same time I started once again growing in the Love, Joy and Peace of the Holy Spirit.

Interesting, once I changed, our relationship changed!

My experience is not unique. We're told by the news outlets that we live in a society filled with stress.

The "world" tells us to "take a pill to relieve the stress." The manufacturer also indicates all the side effects that may happen when we take the pill.

Taking a pill doesn't make sense when you consider the advertised side effects.

But life could be easy:

Do the will of God the Father.

Doing God's will results in Love, Joy and Peace!

Your will—Satan! Stress, envy, anger etc.!

What happened after Jesus left the Garden of Olives?

Jesus is again living fully in the Holy Spirit and has the strength to do His Father's will and submit Himself fully to the Cross.

If you go to christiananswers.net and type in how did Jesus Christ die? The medical answer you will read implies the same question I asked, how did He do it?

Jesus hadn't eaten since the last supper, He sweat blood, He was beaten up by the Jews, scourged, a crown of thorns pushed down on His head, and forced to carry His cross.

How did He do it?

Jesus Is Scourged

I am always amazed when I read the Gospel descriptions of Jesus being scourged.

*Then he released Barabbas to them, **but after he had Jesus scourged,** he handed him over to be crucified.*
(Emphasis mine NABRE Mt 27:26)

*So Pilate, wishing to satisfy the crowd, released Barabbas to them and, after **he had Jesus scourged**, handed him over to be crucified.*
(Emphasis mine NABRE MK 15:15)

Therefore I shall have him flogged and then release him.
(NABRE Lk 23:16)

*Then Pilate took Jesus and **had him scourged.***
(Emphasis mine NABRE Jn 19:1)

Luke said Jesus was flogged, according to the **New American Bible Revised Edition**. Mathew, Mark and John said Jesus was scourged.

He was scourged!

This is basically all that was said in three of the four gospels.

He was scourged!

No other adverbs, just he was scourged.

It wasn't until the movie **The Passion of the Christ** that I more fully understood the torture that Jesus went through.

Scourging used whips with metal hooks on the end of each strand. When the hooks landed on the back of a person, they dug in, and when the whip was pulled back, the hooks took skin with them.

This was a form of torture!

I chose the NRSV (**New Revised Standard Version**) as the primary Bible I would use in writing this book. The NRSV said Jesus was flogged in all four gospels.

I couldn't believe it.

Flogging is a whip which is swung so the middle of the whip lands on the shoulder of a person tied between two posts, and the smaller whips at the end strike the stomach or back. Flogging was a cruel form of punishment, but I don't believe it was as cruel as scourging.

This is a battle, and Satan will use all force necessary to break Jesus.

The Second Sorrowful Mystery of the Rosary, **Scourging at the Pillar,** has claimed for centuries that Jesus was scourged, not flogged.

I must admit I am puzzled by the difference between the NA-BRE and the NRSV. I have a web page that must have 20 different bibles on it, and more than one says Jesus was flogged.

When you consider the whole process of Jesus being put to death as a battle, it becomes clear Satan would scourge Jesus for maximum pain to get Jesus to scream out.

Consider the events so far. Jesus was brought before the Sanhedrin and was NOT convicted by the false testimony of witnesses called to testify against Him.

Satan the father of lies lost!

Jesus was not intimidated by the manhandling and beating He received from the temple guards. Jesus remained silent!

Satan lost!

Satan was not going to let this next opportunity slip by.

Jesus was scourged!

Satan lost. Jesus remained silent.

Waiting for a haircut one day I happened to read in **People Magazine** that the actor, Jim Caviezel, who took the role of Jesus in **The Passion of the Christ**, said they placed a board on his back, and the whip with the metal hooks would hit the board.

On one swing, one of the strands of the whip missed the board and hit Caviezel with the metal claw digging into Jim's back. Jim said the pain that shot through his body was indescribable, Jim couldn't scream because the pain was so intense.

Remember, this was one strand of a whip, not all the strands, and I am also sure it was not pulled back to tear out the skin.

He was oppressed, and he was afflicted,
yet he did not open his mouth;
like a lamb that is led to the slaughter,
and like a sheep that before its shearers is silent,
so he did not open his mouth.
(Is 53:7)

With revilement and torture let us put the just one to the test
that we may have proof of his gentleness and try his patience.
Let us condemn him to a shameful death; for according to his
own words, God will take care of him.
(NABRE Wis 2:19-20)

I am repeating these two Old Testament readings to remind you of the battle that was predicted by Isaiah and in the Book of Wisdom which is now taking place.

With each swing of the whip, Jesus' Gentleness and Patience are tested. I always considered the total process, not each step.

Each step was a chance for victory or defeat on the part of Jesus.

If Jesus screams for mercy during His Scourging, He loses, salvation is lost. Each swing of the whip, then, is a small battle in and of itself.

How many Lents did I say I would do something—stop smoking, for example—and failed on Ash Wednesday, the first day of Lent.

I sadly couldn't even make it for one day.

By concentrating on the Cross, I was finally able to quit smoking after two prior defeats.

I now realize that I was, and still am, in a personal battle with Satan every day, and Victory has to be my objective.

It must have shocked the Roman torturers that Jesus was not screaming for mercy, cursing them or reacting as so many others had before Jesus.

What's going on?

The Roman soldiers aren't swinging easier; they're trying harder to break Jesus.

For Jesus not to acknowledge what they are trying to put Him through is a defeat for them, and they know it.

I have watched **The Passion of the Christ** three times and am always struck at the scene when the Centurion in charge of the scourging tells the guards to stop.

"Are you trying to kill Him?" the Centurion asks.

Yes, they are, and it's because they are losing. Even worse, they know it.

The Roman guards at the end of the scene are bent over exhausted.

They have nothing left!

The Lion of God defeated the Roman soldiers and Satan.

Jesus stayed silent!

'Rabbouni'

Matthew and Mark said Judas identified Jesus at the Mount of Olives by calling Him "Rabbi," which means a distinguished teacher.

at once he came up to Jesus and said, "Greetings Rabbi!" and kissed him.
(Mt 26:49)

he went up to him at once and said, "Rabbi." and kissed him.
(Mk 14:45)

In the Gospel of John, the resurrected Jesus meets Mary of Magdalene outside the tomb, and she asks Him what they have done with the body.

"Whom are you looking for?" Supposing him to be the gardener, she said to him, "Sir, if you have carried him away, tell me where you have laid him, and I will take him away." Jesus said to her, "Mary!" She turned and said to him in Hebrew, "Rab-

bouni"!" (which means Teacher).
(Jn 20:15-16)

Matthew and Mark start the crucifixion process at the Mount of Olives with the title Rabbi (teacher). John, who wrote the last of the four Gospels, wrote that after Jesus rose from the dead, Mary of Magdalene called Jesus "Rabbouni" and John's Gospel defines "Rabbouni" as teacher, so all will know its meaning.

The word teacher appears to me as bookends, and the book they are holding is the Book of Life.

Life in the Holy Spirit!

Jesus Takes Up His Cross

A fter Jesus was scourged, He was forced to take up His Cross.

How did He do it?

I recently read that the average adult has between 1 and 1.5 gallons of blood in their body. How much blood did Jesus lose because of His scourging?

After He was scourged, a Crown of two-inch thorns was placed on his head.

Placed?

They were forced onto His head!

Never forget that during Jesus' Crucifixion, the Roman soldiers are mad as hell that they can't break Jesus.

They are not easing up, they're piling it on.

Have you ever seen a head wound?

Our son David cut his head badly as a child when he fell off a bed he was jumping on and hit his head on the radiator. I was shocked at the amount of blood that flowed from that wound. I wasn't sure we would make it to the hospital in time.

After a few stitches, Dave was fine.

Jesus has a crown of two-inch thorns piercing into His head, which meant an even greater loss of blood.

Jesus, with the forced help of Simon of Cyrene, is made to carry His cross to the "Place of the Skull."

How did He do it?

The loss of blood, and lack of food and water, should have made Him so weak that He couldn't carry His Cross and walk to His death.

Stop reading at this point and spend a few moments considering all Jesus has gone through, and maybe you will also ask, as I have:

How did He do it?

The answer of course is the unseen power of the Holy Spirit.

Outrageous Love!

Jesus, the man, has been physically beaten up.

But!

The energy source that drives Him forward to climb up onto His Cross is His love of His Father and all of mankind.

Love always wins!

Two events stand out to me on His march to Golgotha.

The first event:

Jesus falls three times.

What are we taught by the falls?

Get up!

Life is one step at a time. A marathon is won one step at a time.

I have tended to look for the finish line way before it is in sight.

Because I couldn't see the finish line, I quit!

Quitting smoking is a great example. Satan kept me blind to living in the present, I AM, and just taking that next step: stop smoking today.

Instead, Satan had me look to the future, the finish line, Easter, and as a result, I twice failed to quit smoking, because I didn't believe I could go that long without having another cigarette.

Jesus tells us not to beat ourselves up over our falls.

Get up!

Jesus' example is even more telling because with each fall the Cross comes crushing down upon Him.

As the Cross presses down upon Him, His Crown of Thorns digs deeper into His head.

If I get up, doing God the Father's will, as Jesus did, I will be given the strength by the Holy Spirit to reach my personal Golgotha!

Take the next step!

With each step, Victory!

Never give up!

The second event:

Veronica wipes the face of Jesus.

This is not in the Bible but part of Catholic tradition found in the Stations of the Cross.

The sixth station—*Veronica wipes the face of Jesus.*

Think of the many times you have been in a crowd and you see an injustice. What do you do?

Let me make the question easier. When you are at a parade and the American flag passes by, what do you do?

Stand up, take off your hat, if you're wearing one, and put your hand over your heart?

Or:

Make no acknowledgement of the flag so as not to stand out?

Veronica was moved by what she saw. She was witnessing a man convicted of blasphemy, being led to His death on a cross, treated cruelly by the Roman soldiers, being spit upon and cursed by the crowds that lined the path to Golgotha.

Veronica stepped out from the crowd, ignored the Roman soldiers, and wiped the face of Jesus. Jesus in return left an imprint of His face on her towel.

In thinking about Veronica, isn't this the parable of the Good Samaritan (Lk 10:25-37) taking place in front of all the people there, and now for us?

She couldn't stop Jesus from being crucified.

She couldn't carry His Cross.

She could wipe His face.

I am sure that her act of Love also gave Jesus extra strength to continue putting one step in front of the other.

"Why?" you might ask.

Jesus' compassion for the lowly is being given in return to Jesus by Veronica imitating Jesus.

Interesting!

Veronica is acting as Jesus did when he healed the sick and fed the hungry, and now Jesus was the recipient of her compassion.

Veronica, in my mind, also raises other interesting questions.

Where are the men?

Answer: They're crucifying Him!

Where were all the people who were healed?

Answer: I don't know.

Where were the 5,000 whom Jesus fed?

Answer: Once again I don't know.

Only Veronica was left to offer physical comfort to Jesus.

A woman who imitated Jesus!

Jesus Is Nailed to the Cross

J esus arrives at Golgotha and is stripped of His clothing and nailed to the Cross.

Most people have never thought of how Jesus died.

Crucifixion was designed to be so devilishly intense that one would continually long for death, but could linger for days with no relief.

Furthermore, the position of the body on a cross is designed to make it extremely difficult to breathe. (Christananswers.net)

When a person is crucified, the weight of the body forces the chest cavity to gradually collapse into the lungs. The person being crucified would force their body up by pushing up on their feet in order to keep breathing.

The Roman guards knew this. They first drove nails that were 6 to 8 inches long into His wrists. There is a tendon that extends from the wrist to the shoulder. When the nail was driven into the wrist, the tendon would tear and break, forcing Jesus to use His back muscles to support Him so that He could breathe.

Next, His feet were crossed and both feet nailed with a single nail, impaling His feet to the Cross.

He was forced to alternate between arching His back and using His legs to continue breathing.

Imagine the struggle taking place.

When I look at paintings or drawings of Jesus Crucified, I see three men crucified but in many of the paintings, the men on the right and left are tied to their crosses.

Jesus is nailed!

Why?

Yes, the Jews said "Crucify Him," but did that mean nail Him to the Cross?

Question:

Since Jesus didn't break while he was being scourged, were the Roman soldiers using this one last opportunity to continue to try to break Jesus?

This was a battle in which no quarter was given!

Jesus would scream for mercy!

Up to this point, the Roman soldiers had been beaten by Jesus and they knew it!

This is where being a Christian is so positive.

Look to the Cross!

Every time I say I can't do something, I think of Jesus on the Cross.

If Jesus could climb up on the Cross and hang there for three hours, then I can use Him as my teacher, and do what I have to do to change my life.

Every Lent, I make changes in my life.

As I grow older, this has become easier because I realize if I use Jesus' death on the Cross as my motivator, I can't fail.

When Satan whispers for me to give up, I think of God's Lion on His Cross and tell Satan to "get behind me," and I continue on with my change.

When Lent is over, I try not to go back to the habits I gave up that Lent. I continue on and celebrate the change that Lent has brought into my life.

Jesus Hangs on the Cross

F or three hours Jesus hung on the Cross, slowly suffocating to death.

A horrible death!

If you watched **The Passion of the Christ**, or for that matter any movie showing Jesus' death on the Cross, we see only the physical side of that death.

I think—in fact, I am sure—other elements were also taking place.

As Jesus was dying, He lived fully in the Fruit of the Holy Spirit. Jesus lived in Love, Joy and Peace.

"How is that possible?" you might ask.

In our first book, **A Journey with the Holy Spirit**, I discuss in great detail the Fruit of the Holy Spirit and how we can all grow in the Fruit of the Holy Spirit.

Briefly, the Fruit of the Holy Spirit is defined by Saint Paul in Galatians 5:22-23 as Love, Joy, Peace, Patience, Kindness, Generosity, Faithfulness, Gentleness and Self-Control.

You and I grow in the Love, Joy and Peace of the Holy Spirit by practicing and growing in Patience, Kindness, Generosity, Faithfulness, Gentleness and Self-Control.

Think of your own life. Every time you gave of yourself, Generosity, doesn't a feeling of Joy fill your spirit?

Of course it does!

Joy is the result of an increase of Love brought about by your Generosity to that person.

The question, then, is how can I increase and grow in Love, Joy and Peace?

Pray for an increase in Patience, Kindness, Generosity, Faithfulness, Gentleness and Self-Control.

Let's examine the six Fruit that led to Jesus' living and dying in Love, Joy and Peace.

PATIENCE:

"Patience" implies suffering, enduring or waiting, as a determination of the will and not simply under necessity. As such it is an essential Christian virtue to the exercise of which there are many exhortations. We need to "wait patiently" for God, to endure uncomplainingly the various forms of sufferings, wrongs and evils that we meet with, and to bear patiently injustices which we cannot remedy and provocations we cannot remove. (Biblestudytools.com)

The crucifixion process starts at the Last Supper. Let's just say that was about 6 p.m. on Thursday evening. According to St. Luke, Jesus died at 3 p.m. This is a period of about 21 hours. He hung on the Cross with nails driven through His precious body until 3 in the afternoon. (Lk 23: 44).

Jesus is the Son of God!

He could have had an arrow shot through His heart. That would have resulted in His death, and He would have bled, but His death would have been quick, and what would have been taught?

Not Patience!

Patience takes time.

Remember, Jesus, "Rabbouni," was teaching us from His Cross. We are to take these lessons and apply them to our lives and our own crosses.

Grow in Patience, do the will of God the Father, and all will work out to His, God the Father's, glory.

Notice I did not say your glory. We are here to glorify God the Father, through His Son in the Holy Spirit.

Jesus spent nine months in Mary's womb. He lived 30 years as a carpenter, and three years as a teacher. If He had died in that 33-year period, I believe we would never have known about Him.

Why?

What Jesus said and did, others said and did before Him.

Some examples of this are:

Jesus walked on the water.
(Mt 14:25)

Moses parted the Red Sea and wiped out the Egyptian Army.
(Ex 14:15-30)

Elijah and Elisha parted the Jordan River and walked across on dry land.
(2 Ki 2: 8 & 14)

Jesus fed 5,000 with two fish and five loaves of bread.
(Lk 13:17)

Elijah fed a woman and her son for many days from a jar of flour and a jug of oil.
(1 Ki 17:14-15)

Jesus raised at least three people from the dead.
(Lk 7:15-49; Jn 12:17 Mt 9:24)

Elijah raised the son of the widow of Zarephath from the dead.
(1 Ki 17:20-22).

In my youth, I believed that what Jesus did was totally unique to Jesus. You can imagine my surprise as I read the Bible, and discovered other Prophets had performed somewhat similar miracles.

What makes Jesus unique, then, was His death.

A just Man died for the unjust. He allowed the process to take place over a period of time.

KINDNESS:

Divine Kindness, God's kindness, is presupposed or taught throughout Scripture. It is manifest in what is called "common

grace." God is kind to all He has made (Psalm 145:9), even when His creatures are ungrateful and wicked (Luke 6:35; Matt 5:45). His kindness is intended to lead to repentance, not to rejection of Him (Rom 2:4).
(Google Biblical definition of Kindness)

The criminal on Jesus' right asks Jesus to remember him:

But the other rebuked him, saying, "Do you not fear God, since you are under the same sentence of condemnation? And we indeed have been condemned justly, for we are getting what we deserve for our deeds, but this man has done nothing wrong." Then he said, "Jesus, remember me when you come into your kingdom." He replied, "Truly I tell you, today you will be with me in Paradise."
(Lk 23:40-43)

Both men confessed Jesus as being the Messiah. Both made a request—one to save his skin, the other to be remembered, that's all, just remember me. He probably didn't dare to ask for more. He, according to his own testimony, was justly being put to death for his actions.

He, a criminal, asked not to be forgotten. He asked because he must have believed that he had a chance to be forgiven.

Not only is he forgiven, but he is told that he will be with Jesus in Paradise.

When?

Today!

Outrageous Love!

The criminal on the right is the prodigal son being welcomed home by the Father, Jesus and The Holy Spirit! (Lk 15: 11-32)

The criminal on the right is the lost sheep, which Jesus went out to find and brought back on His shoulders. (Lk 15:3-7)

Jesus could have said, "Sometime in the near future, you will be with me in Paradise."

Or:

"You're a criminal. You expect to be remembered based on what you just told me?"

I read **Glimpses of Heaven** by Trudy Harris, a hospice nurse who told of last-minute conversions to Jesus by people on their death bed.

And?

The question that begs to be asked is: Didn't that person who waited until the last minute to find Jesus win?

Didn't they beat the system?

After all, he or she lived a life in the "world" doing their will, not living in the Holy Spirit, and now in the last hours of their life, they find Jesus.

They're going to Heaven!

Earlier in my life, I asked myself this very question:

Why not wait until my last days on earth and then convert? I will live in the "world," chase all its pleasures (?), and on my deathbed find Jesus.

The brother of the Prodigal Son asked the opposite question:

Now the older son had been out in the field and, on his way back, as he neared the house, he heard the sound of music and dancing. He called one of the servants and asked what this

might mean. The servant said to him, "Your brother has returned and your father has slaughtered the fattened calf because he has him back safe and sound." He became angry, and when he refused to enter the house, his father came out and pleaded with him. He said to his father in reply, **"Look, all these years I served you and not once did I disobey your orders; yet you never gave me even a young goat to feast on with my friends.** *But when your son returns who swallowed up your property with prostitutes, for him you slaughter the fattened calf." He said to him,* **"My son, you are here with me always; everything I have is yours. But now we must celebrate and rejoice, because your brother was dead and has come to life again; he was lost and has been found."**
(Emphasis mine NAB Lk 15: 25-32)

Early in my life, I thought as the older brother in the above Parable. The sinner has to pay for his sins!

Retribution was required!

What's in it for me for being loyal every day?

Why not live in the "world" with all its pleasures (?)?

His brother, the Prodigal Son, sinned, and is now welcomed back with a big party!

It's not fair!

What I never considered:

God is a God of Outrageous Love, and aren't I asked to imitate God?

Yes, I am!

More importantly, don't I want to be the recipient of that Outrageous Love?

Yes, I do!

After all, in the eyes of God, and in my eyes, I am a sinner!

I sadly was a Prodigal Son, which I spoke of in **A Journey with the Holy Spirit**.

I cry when I realize all I have missed by not doing the Father's will and listening to the whisper of the Holy Spirit in my younger years.

Life could have been a lot richer. Richer is an interesting word as I think about it. Money no - Joy and Peace ABSOLUTLY!

This question shows a complete lack of knowledge on my part, of the fantastic life that is available by living in the Holy Spirit.

Thank God I found, and now try to live, in the "Spirit World!"

Yes, I believe the person who waits until the last moment will be justified, and be with Jesus in Paradise. The man on Jesus' right tells us this.

But!

I am also certain they lived a life not knowing and growing in the Love, Joy and Peace of the Holy Spirit.

A far better lifestyle!

The Holy Spirit reminded me of the parable of the Laborers in the Vineyard.

*For the kingdom of heaven is like a **landowner who went** out early in the morning to hire laborers for his vineyard. After agreeing with the laborers for the usual daily wage, he sent them into his vineyard. When **he went out** about nine o'clock, he saw others standing idle in the marketplace; and he said to them, "You also go into the vineyard, and I will pay you what-*

ever is right." So they went. When **he went out** *again about noon and about three o'clock, he did the same. And about five o'clock* **he went out** *and found others standing around; and he said to them, "Why are you standing here idle all day?" They said to him, "Because no one has hired us." He said to them, "You also go into the vineyard." When evening came, the owner of the vineyard said to his manager, "Call the laborers and give them their pay, beginning with the last and then going to the first." When those hired about five o'clock came, each of them received the usual daily wage. Now when the first came, they thought they would receive more; but each of them also received the usual daily wage. And when they received it, they grumbled against the landowner, saying, "These last worked only one hour, and you have made them equal to us who have borne the burden of the day and the scorching heat." But he replied to one of them, "Friend, I am doing you no wrong; did you not agree with me for the usual daily wage? Take what belongs to you and go; I choose to give to this last the same as I give to you. Am I not allowed to do what I choose with what belongs to me? Or are you envious because I am generous?" So the last will be first, and the first will be last.*
(Emphasis mine Mt 20:1-16)

Notice:

The owner always went out to get the workers.

The first to be hired were promised the usual daily wage.

The men hired around noon were promised to be paid what was right.

I'm sure they thought, "Half a day's pay is better than none."

The last to be hired were told to go into the vineyard. No mention of pay.

The men who were hired in the morning knew they would earn enough money to buy food for that day (daily wage), and this knowledge gave them Joy and Peace as they worked in the fields.

Tonight they would eat!

The men who were chosen first represent those who have lived most or all of their lives in the "Spirit World."

I was like the men who were hired at noon. I truly discovered God at age 40.

The first half of the day, they worried they wouldn't have money to buy food for the day, and lived the first part of the day in stress.

When they were hired, I am sure they felt a half a loaf is better than none. They probably would still have some stress as they worked, but not as much.

When the laborers who worked half a day were paid a full day's wage, they were filled with Joy, for it was much more than they had expected.

The men hired last didn't know until they were paid if they would earn enough to eat even a small amount of food that day.

They could've said, "No, I'm not going to work for you," and their thinking would be, "How much could the owner pay me for an hour's work?"

"It's not worth it."

When you consider it, isn't the real question: Why did they work?

Once the last to be hired were paid the full daily wage, they were filled with a greater Joy, for by worldly standards they were grossly overpaid.

But!

They spent that day worried that they would not have any money to buy food. Consider also this might not be the first day they had missed a meal.

Who else has demonstrated this type of Love?

I can't think of anyone, and yet, of all places, Kindness is being taught from the Cross, by Jesus while He is being crucified.

GENEROSITY:

Jesus gave it all, His blood and water. He emptied Himself fully.

So many times I thought I will do whatever it is that is being asked of me and not look for anything in return.

It never happens!

I am filled with Joy.

Joy!

With this in mind, I think of Jesus on the Cross.

Then Jesus said, "Father, forgive them; for they do not know what they are doing."
(Lk 23:34)

This is the ultimate gift of Outrageous Love from God the Father through Jesus, filled with the Holy Spirit, to you and I— the ones who drove the nails into His precious Hands and Feet, by our sins.

With this ultimate gift of Generosity, Jesus continues to live in Love, Joy and Peace.

FAITHFULNESS:

Do you not believe that I am in the Father and the Father is in me? The words that I say to you I do not speak on my own; but the Father who dwells in me does his works.
(Jn 14:10)

Jesus always did His Father's will. We are asked to do the same. This is why we claim He never sinned.

Why is it so hard to do the will of God the Father?

Satan!

Satan presents living in the "world," not the Holy Spirit, as a better alternative.

Some examples are: Becoming famous, making piles of money for my enjoyment, cheating on your wife and family, forgetting the poor (it's their fault anyway), cheating on your taxes. The list goes on and on.

Following Jesus and doing His Father's will is presented by Satan as, dull ... hard ... not possible ... as I was led to believe for so many years.

Satan!

And sadly, I listened to Satan.

When we pray the Our Father, we say **Thy**, God the Father's, **will be done, on earth**, where it's not, **as it is in heaven**, where it is.

We also pray **Thy Kingdom come**.

When?

Here and now!

You don't see any asterisk after the word come with a footnote saying not now but later.

If we do the will of God the Father, would we be in Heaven now?

Yes—Jesus on the Cross—Filled with Love, Joy and Peace.

Yes—But Heaven on earth entails a continuing battle with Satan; Heaven after we die doesn't.

Having been disciplined a little, they will receive great good,
because God tested them and found them worthy of himself;
like gold in the furnace he tried them,
and like a sacrificial burnt offering he accepted them.
In the time of their visitation they will shine forth,
and will run like sparks through the stubble.
They will govern nations and rule over peoples,
and the Lord will reign over them forever.
Those who trust in him will understand truth,
and the faithful will abide with him in love,
because grace and mercy are upon his holy ones,
and he watches over his elect.
(NABRE Wis 3:5-9)

Heaven as defined in the book of Wisdom.

Life is full of crosses. Everyone has them. No one escapes. The choice we have to make, then, is: Live in the "world," which is full of stress, hatred, envy, lust, addictions to alcohol or drugs etc.

Or:

Live in the Holy Spirit. Live in the Love, Joy and Peace, doing the will of God the Father.

Choose to be Faithful as Jesus was Faithful to God our Father even while hanging on the Cross.

GENTLENESS:

In Matthew 11:29, Christ said, "Take My yoke upon you and learn from Me, for I am gentle and lowly in heart, and you will find rest for your souls." Here Christ makes a connection between gentleness and humility.
(Google Fruit of the Spirit: Gentleness)

*With revilement and torture let us put the just one to the test that we may have proof of his gentleness
and try his patience.
Let us condemn him to a shameful death.*
(NABRE Wis 2:19-20)

Jesus didn't rebuke the man on His right, He welcomed Him into Paradise.

He didn't condemn the Romans who drove the Nails into His body, He forgave them.

Jesus didn't avoid His Cross, He welcomed it. Through His death, all men might be justified.

Jesus humbled Himself and allowed Himself to be stripped naked, nailed and hung on the Cross for three hours while many around Him taunted Him.

All of this Jesus did to establish the Gentleness of Father, Son and Holy Spirit.

SELF-CONTROL:

He was oppressed, and he was afflicted,
yet he did not open his mouth;
like a lamb that is led to the slaughter,
and like a sheep that before its shearers is silent,
so he did not open his mouth.
(Is. 53:7)

Isaiah said this is how Jesus would die.

Like a Lamb!

This is how He did die.

Like a Lamb.

Thank you Jesus!

In my life, Self-Control has been a big issue, as I related in **A Journey with the Holy Spirit.**

Recently I was at a stoplight and the person in the car in front of me didn't start up fast enough.

I exploded!

"Where did that come from?" I asked myself.

Satan!

I was surprised, shocked and saddened that I had exploded and lost for a moment my Self-Control.

This is not the person I want to be.

I thought I had grown in Self-Control.

Immediately I said I was sorry, and like Jesus falling while He carried His Cross, I picked myself up and started in again, putting one foot in front of the other, trying to live my life in the Holy Spirit.

I have told this story because I have found life is like golf. Every time I feel I have the game down, it falls apart.

The only answer is never getting self-confident and stop living in the "Spirit World."

Stay and grow in the Self-Control of the Holy Spirit.

Jesus Dies on the Cross

I was talking with Msgr. Henchal one day about this book, and he told me that Muslims believe Jesus did not die, and even more interesting didn't die on the Cross.

The Muslim apologist and author Ahmed Deedat agrees, "On the subject of the crucifixion, the Muslim is told in no uncertain terms in the Holy Qur'an ... that they did not kill Him, nor did they crucify Him." Therefore the Qur'anic teaching is clearly that Jesus did not die by crucifixion, which is in direct contrast to Christianity, which says there is no salvation apart from the cross (Mt. 26:28; Mk. 14:22-24; cf. 1 Cor. 1:18). Putting all theological beliefs aside, what does the evidence suggest? Did Jesus really die by crucifixion or did he just appear dead? (CARM.org, Islam and the Crucifixion of Jesus)

I was stunned.

Researching Msgr. Henchal's statement, further I discovered:

*According to the Quran, Jesus, although appearing to have
been crucified, was not killed by crucifixion or by any other
means; instead, "God raised him unto Himself." **Like all
prophets in Islam.***
(Emphasis mine, Wikipedia)

This might be true if one didn't take into account the brutality
of the Roman Army.

Once again I was talking with Msgr. Henchal about why Jesus
had to be Crucified and how we know He died on the Cross. He
asked me if I knew what the word DECIMATES meant.

I had no idea.

*Decimation (Latin: decimatio; decem = "ten") was a form of
military discipline used by senior commanders in the Roman
Army to punish units or large groups guilty of capital offences
such as mutiny or desertion. The word decimation is derived
from Latin meaning "removal of a tenth." The procedure was a
pragmatic attempt to balance the need to punish serious offences with the practicalities of dealing with a large group of
offenders.*

*Procedure
A cohort (roughly 480 soldiers) selected for punishment by
decimation was divided into groups of ten; each group drew
lots (Sortation), and the soldier on whom the lot fell was executed by his nine comrades, often by stoning or clubbing. The
remaining soldiers were often given rations of barley instead of
wheat (the latter being the standard soldier's diet) for a few
days, and required to camp outside the fortified security of the
marching camp.*

*Because the punishment fell by lot, all soldiers in the group
were eligible for execution, regardless of the individual degree
of fault, or rank and distinction, unless rigged to eliminate the
mutiny ringleaders. The leadership was usually executed inde-*

pendently of the one in ten deaths of the rank and file.
(Wikipedia)

The Roman Centurion who was in charge of the crucifixion knew if any of the three men they had just crucified survived, they would be put to death.

I refer you to the Acts of the Apostles after Peter was freed from jail by an Angel.

*When Herod had searched for him and could not find him, he examined the guards and **ordered them to be put to death.***
(Emphasis mine Ac 12:19)

The Centurion knew when he reported back to Pilate he needed to qualify to Pilate, that the three men were in fact dead.

But when they came to Jesus and saw that he was already dead, they did not break his legs. Instead, one of the soldiers pierced his side with a spear, and at once blood and water came out. (He who saw this has testified so that you also may believe. His testimony is true, and he knows that he tells the truth.)
(Jn 19: 33-34)

Self-preservation of the Centurion and the guards made them take the extra step of insuring all three men were dead.

The Holy Spirit then directed my thoughts to St. Thomas.

But Thomas (who was called the Twin), one of the 12, was not with them when Jesus came. So the other disciples told him, "We have seen the Lord." But he said to them, "Unless I see the mark of the nails in his hands, and put my finger in the mark of the nails and my hand in his side, I will not believe."

A week later his disciples were again in the house and Thomas was with them. Although the doors were shut, Jesus came and

stood among them and said, "Peace be with you." Then he said to Thomas, "Put your finger here and see my hands. Reach out your hand and put it in my side. Do not doubt but believe." Thomas answered him, "My Lord and my God!"
(Jn 20:24-28)

Now, the most beautiful prayer resulting from Thomas' doubt:

Jesus said to him, "Have you believed because you have seen me? **Blessed are those who have not seen and yet have come to believe."**
(Emphasis mine Jn 20:29)

The Outrageous Love of God for Thomas, the one who denied His rising from the dead, and us.

I have separated this into two sections.

First: Thomas said he wouldn't believe.

Why?

He knew Jesus was fully human, was crucified, and had died. Thomas had been there when Jesus raised a girl and later Lazarus from the dead.

He couldn't believe that Jesus would be raised from the dead. How is that possible?

Good question.

Jesus was DEAD!

Who, or what person, would raise Him?

His Father! (Gal 1:1)

Jesus asked Thomas to examine the wounds that Thomas knew had been inflicted on Jesus. When Thomas saw the wounds, he replied, *"My Lord and my God."*

If Jesus had been stoned, as St. Stephen was, this whole scene would not have taken place.

Except in Matthew's Gospel (Mt 28:9), Jesus was not recognized by anyone when He first appeared to people after His Resurrection.

It was the nail marks in His hands and feet and the mark the spear left in His side that identified Jesus to His followers.

After Jesus rose from the dead His appearance changed.

If Jesus had been stoned, it would have been easy, then, to say He, Jesus, hadn't died.

Go to Acts:

But Jews came there from Antioch and Iconium and won over the crowds. Then they stoned Paul and dragged him out of the city, supposing that he was dead. But when the disciples surrounded him, he got up and went into the city. The next day he went on with Barnabas to Derbe.
(Ac 14:19-20)

The key words: *supposing that he was dead.*

Wait a second!

Maybe you're thinking, as I thought for so many years, they didn't use big stones, or they missed in their throws.

No!

The Jews meant to kill Paul!

They hated Paul!

I don't believe they supposed they killed him, they knew they killed him.

And dragged him out of the city.

The Bible said his *disciples surrounded him.*

I have to believe his disciples prayed over him, not just *surrounded him.*

Do you really think they stood around and said, "Poor Paul, I told him to quiet down or something like this would happen."

These are Paul's disciples; their first instinct would be to pray for Paul. They had seen the power of prayer while they were with Paul.

Paul came back to life.

I recently read the book **90 Minutes in Heaven: A True Story of Death and Life,** by Don Piper. Don was ruled dead for 90 minutes by the paramedics who came to the site of his automobile accident.

He was prayed over by a Baptist minister.

He came back to life!

Prayers worked back in the early days of the church and work now!

But!

The question that could always be asked is, "Did Paul and Don actually die?" Someone who doesn't believe would answer, "No, Paul and Don didn't die."

As the old saying goes, "For the believer, no proof is needed. For the non-believer, no amount of proof is sufficient."

When you consider the death and resurrection of Jesus as a battle, God the Father's battle plan was exquisite.

Why Didn't They Break Jesus' Legs?

In John's gospel, written decades after Jesus is Crucified, John quotes Psalm 34: 20:

"None of his bones shall be broken."
(Jn 19:36)

Question:

Why didn't they break the legs of Jesus as they did to the criminals on Jesus' left and right?

When the centurion saw what had taken place, he praised God and said, "Certainly this man was innocent."
(Lk 23: 47)

Jesus was dead, and in His death Jesus had soundly defeated the Romans.

Jesus died in Love, Joy and Peace!

He forgave the Romans!

The Centurion knew they had been beaten.

I don't believe this Centurion, or any other Centurion for that matter, had experienced a man being Crucified asking His Father to forgive them, the Roman soldiers, who are crucifying Him.

"For they know not what they are doing."
(Lk 23:34)

As an act of respect, the Centurion ordered that a lance be thrust into the side of Jesus.

I am positive the Centurion ordered a lance be thrust into the side of Jesus because of my two years of service in the U.S. Navy.

I was ordered to do what I was supposed to do. They didn't give me a choice, or ask my opinion.

If I wanted to stay out of the brig (jail), I did as I was ordered.

The Centurion would not allow any further mutilation of the body of Jesus to take place.

They were beaten!

The lance thrust into the side of Jesus had to take place so the Centurion could report back to Pilate that all three men were in fact dead, and how he knew for sure they were dead if asked by Pilate.

Jesus died on the Cross!

If the Centurion had broken Jesus' legs, then it could be claimed that Jesus didn't really die on the Cross.

Jesus hadn't suffocated!

When men of character are in battle, and one side is defeated, the winner shows respect to the vanquished.

Jesus showed that respect by forgiving the Centurion and his men, and you and I.

The Lion of God won, and the Roman Centurion knew it!

'God Will Take Care of Him'

As I continued writing this book, the nagging thought of how did God take care of Jesus kept coming back to me.

With violence and torture let us put the just one to the test
that we may have proof of his gentleness
and try his patience.
Let us condemn him to a shameful death;
for according to his own words, God will take care of him.
(Emphasis mine NAB Wis 2:19-20)

Consider: If we believe the statement *with violence and torture let us put* the just one to the test is true, and I would call the scourging at the pillar, a crowning of thorns and being nailed to the Cross as violence and torture.

And if we believe Jesus is the Just One, and He is,

Then the last statement, *God will take care of Him,* also has to be true!

The Bible can't be correct in two places and wrong in another.

This is not the first time the Bible mentions God helping, providing or taking care of someone:

Abraham took the wood of the burnt offering and laid it on his son Isaac, and he himself carried the fire and the knife. So the two of them walked on together. Isaac said to his father Abraham, "Father!" And he said, "Here I am, my son." He said, "The fire and the wood are here, but where is the lamb for a burnt offering?" Abraham said, **"God himself will provide** *the lamb for a burnt offering, my son."*
(Emphasis mine Gen 22:6-8)

I gave my back to those who struck me,
and my cheeks to those who pulled out the beard;
I did not hide my face
from insult and spitting.
The Lord God helps me;
therefore I have not been disgraced.
(Emphasis mine Isiah 50:6-7)

It was how God provides, helps and takes care of Him I couldn't answer.

In my mind, I questioned the statement, "God will take care of Him." Earlier in the book I wrote, "Yes, God did take care of Him," but I really had no idea of how, and more importantly, how this might imply for us.

Jesus had been scourged, a crown of thorns pushed down on His head, and He was Crucified.

I saw the whole process from a "worldly" prospective, not a Spirit-filled prospective.

I saw the obvious pain and couldn't comprehend how the pain was changed.

No one would claim he didn't die in agony. How else could it have been after being scourged, a crown of thorns forced on His head, and nails driven through His hands and feet?

Or:

Could it possibly be that living in the Holy Spirit, doing the will of God the Father, and not living in the "world," really changes everything?

This is the hardest part of this book I have had to write.

In our first book, **A Journey with the Holy Spirit**, I said Jesus died in the Love, Joy and Peace of the Holy Spirit.

Question:

If Jesus is filled with Love for and from God the Father, Holy Spirit, and Love for the men who are crucifying Him, the Romans, you and I, does the pain inflicted on Him somehow change?

This, to me, has been a very important question, because I have a hard time with the image of God the Father looking down as His Precious Son is filled with pain.

But God the Father didn't look down on Jesus. God the Father was in Jesus, and Jesus was in the Father. (Jn 14:10)

I said looking down to be dramatic.

God the Father wouldn't let His Son be filled with pain!

The answer, then, is living in the Holy Spirit. Living in the "Spirit World," while doing the will of God the Father, changes everything.

Let's look at a few examples.

First example:

From the Old Testament:

Because the king's command was urgent and the furnace was so overheated, the raging flames killed the men who lifted Shadrach, Meshach, and Abednego. But the three men, Shadrach, Meshach, and Abednego, fell down, bound, into the furnace of blazing fire.

Then King Nebuchadnezzar was astonished and rose up quickly. He said to his counselors, "Was it not three men that we threw bound into the fire?" They answered the king, "True, O king." He replied, "But I see four men unbound, walking in the middle of the fire, and they are not hurt; and the fourth has the appearance of a god." Nebuchadnezzar then approached the door of the furnace of blazing fire and said, "Shadrach, Meshach, and Abednego, servants of the Most High God, come out! Come here!" So Shadrach, Meshach, and Abednego came out from the fire. **And the satraps, the prefects, the governors, and the king's counselors gathered together and saw that the fire had not had any power over the bodies of those men; the hair of their heads was not singed, their tunics were not harmed, and not even the smell of fire came from them.** *(Emphasis mine Da 3: 22-27)*

As I read the Bible I find God to be a God of surprises! I also now realize he took care of Shadrach, Meshach, and Abednego.

John Pollock, the author of **The Apostle: The Life of Paul** wrote concerning Christian martyrs at the time of St. Paul:

"In the midst of the flame and rack," wrote Seneca, "I have seen men not only not groan, that is little: not only not complain, that is little, not only not answer back, that too is little; **but I have seen them smile, and smile with a good heart.***"*

Keep Seneca's last words, **"but I have seen them smile, and smile with a good heart."** in mind as you read the next examples.

The New Testament:

When they had called in the apostles, they had them flogged. Then they ordered them not to speak in the name of Jesus, and let them go. As they left the council, **they rejoiced** *that they were considered worthy to suffer dishonor for the sake of the name. And every day in the temple and at home they did not cease to teach and proclaim Jesus as the Messiah.*
(Emphasis mine Ac 5: 40-42)

The Apostles were brought before the council, and when they refused the demand by the council to stop talking about Jesus, they were flogged!

God the Father took care of the apostles!

They left rejoicing!

Wait—their backs have just been ripped open from a flogging, and they're rejoicing?

It would be one thing to have endured the flogging without making a sound, but to leave rejoicing?

They also went back into the temple and repeated doing what they were just flogged for, without fear of more floggings.

This doesn't make any sense, at least not to people who choose to live in the "world."

If you live in the Holy Spirit, it makes complete sense.

Next example:

*After they had given them a **severe flogging,** they threw them into prison and ordered the jailer to keep them securely. Following these instructions, he put them in the innermost cell and fastened their feet in the stocks.*

About midnight Paul and Silas were praying and singing hymns to God, and the prisoners were listening to them. Suddenly there was an earthquake, so violent that the foundations of the prison were shaken; and immediately all the doors were opened and everyone's chains were unfastened. When the jailer woke up and saw the prison doors wide open, he drew his sword and was about to kill himself, since he supposed that the prisoners had escaped. But Paul shouted in a loud voice, "Do not harm yourself, for we are all here." The jailer called for lights, and rushing in, he fell down trembling before Paul and Silas. Then he brought them outside and said, "Sirs, what must I do to be saved?" They answered, "Believe on the Lord Jesus, and you will be saved, you and your household." They spoke the word of the Lord to him and to all who were in his house. At the same hour of the night he took them and washed their wounds; then he and his entire family were baptized without delay. He brought them up into the house and set food before them; and he and his entire household rejoiced that he had become a believer in God.
(Emphasis mine Ac 16:23-34)

God the Father took care of Paul and Silas.

They were "severely flogged" and in jail praying and singing hymns?

An earthquake occurs, the doors are thrown open and they stay?

This is not how a "worldly" man operates!

Fools, the doors are open!

Get out!

Also notice that because of Paul's and Silas's actions, walking the walk, the jailer instead of falling on his sword, asks to have his family converted.

Why?

The eyes are the window to the soul, and Paul's and Silas' eyes were filled with Love, Joy and Peace.

Not hatred for the people who had unjustly flogged them, or for the jailer who jailed them.

The jailer wanted the same life Paul and Silas lived while in the jail, after being unjustly punished.

He wanted a better life for himself and his family.

Don't we all?

Or do we?

Am I willing to change everything?

Back to the Cross:

Two criminals are crucified beside Jesus, one on His left and one on His right.

The criminal on the left of Jesus kept deriding Him and saying, *"Are you not the Messiah? Save yourself and us!"* (Luke 23:39)

Now that's a "worldly" human response we all understand.

This is not what Paul and Silas did, but this is what those who choose to live in the "world" would do.

Save Yourself and save us!

Not the rest of the world, just us.

When you think about it, you really see how small and petty living in the "world" can be.

Now we have a better idea why the jailer wanted a complete change for himself and his family.

Okay, you're probably thinking "That's the bible," and the eleven Apostles and Paul are unique, but how about later on in years?

Does God take care of us?

Saint Lawrence:

Two years after I stopped working on this book, my mind went blank. In my mind was a quote I had heard and didn't know how to find it. Fr. Paul Stefanko, at daily Mass, told of the death of St. Lawrence, the Saint for that day being grilled slowly on a pan for maximum pain. Saint Lawrence said;

"You may turn me over, I'm done on this side."

This was the quote I was looking for.

Like Jesus on the Cross, St. Lawrence defeated his torturers through Love.

When I heard these words I knew I was going back to work.

The Tradition of Saint Lawrence:

The Prefect of Rome, a greedy pagan, thought the Church had a great fortune hidden away. So he ordered Lawrence to bring the Church's treasure to him. The Saint said he would, in three days. Then he went through the city and gathered together all the poor and sick people supported by the Church. When he showed them to the Prefect, he said: "This is the Church's treasure!"

*In great anger, the Prefect condemned Lawrence to a slow, cruel death. The Saint was tied on top of an iron grill over a slow fire that roasted his flesh little by little, **but Lawrence was burning with so much love of God that he almost did not feel the flames.** In fact, God gave him so much strength and joy that he even joked. **"Turn me over,"** he **said to the judge. "I'm done on this side!" And just before he died, he said, "It's cooked enough now."** (Emphasis mine, Catholic Online)

A "worldly" person would not say "Turn me over; I'm cooked enough now."

St. Lawrence *burned with so much love of God that he almost did not feel the flames.*

Saint Maximilian Kolbe:

At the end of July three prisoners disappeared from the camp, Auschwitz, prompting the deputy camp commander to pick 10 men to be starved to death in an underground bunker to deter further escape attempts. When one of the selected men, Franceszek Gajowniczek, cried out, "My wife!, My Children!," Kolbe volunteered to take his place.

According to eye witnesses, an assistant janitor at the time, in his prison cell, Kolbe led the prisoners in prayer to Our Lady. **Each time the guards checked on him, he was standing or kneeling in the middle of the cell and looking calmly at those who entered.** *After two weeks of dehydration and starvation, only Kolbe remained alive. The guards wanted the bunker emptied, so they gave Kolbe a lethal injection of carbonic acid. Kolbe is said to have raised his arm and* **calmly** *waited for the deadly injection.*
(Emphasis mine Wikipedia, Maximilian Kolbe)

Without food and water the average person would survive complete starvation for a week to ten days. Kolbe was still standing and kneeling while he prayed two weeks after his ordeal started.

Everyone else in the bunker is dead.

Notice Kolbe was at Peace. Like St. Paul and Silas, Kolbe used his time in the bunker to lead the others in prayer.

Who was Kolbe imitating?

Jesus on the Cross!

God the Father took care of St. Maximillian Kolbe, he Kolbe was in Peace.

In my own life, I pray daily for an increase in the Fruit of the Holy Spirit. Since I started this prayer 20 years ago, I fell twice and hit my head hard on the pavement.

I should explain, arthritis has fused my neck and back. When I hit the pavement, my head took the full force of the fall. Thank God I didn't break my neck.

God took care of me!

Both times I got up thanking God the Father, and then started laughing.

Laughing?

I had a hard fall, hitting my head on the pavement! I thanked God for the fall, and laughed.

The pain changed.

I hurt, but not the same way I would have hurt before I started praying for an increase in the Fruit of the Holy Spirit.

After much thought about these two falls, I also realized that if I had cursed after I fell, as I would have done before praying for an increase in the Fruit of The Holy Spirit, my cursing would have amplified the pain.

Yes, God the Father took care of me after my falls!

What I just realized was, if I hadn't had these two falls and rose thanking God the Father and laughing, this chapter would never have been written. How could I write about that which I hadn't experienced?

Interesting how God works in our lives.

I am repeating Seneca's quote because it was made by a non-Christian who was amazed at what he witnessed.

"In the midst of the flame and rack," wrote Seneca, "I have seen men not only not groan, that is little: not only not complain, that is little, not only not answer back, that too is little; **but I have seen them smile, and smile with a good heart."**

I also have read over the years of men enduring very painful deaths and not groan, complain, nor answer back. What made many of the Christian martyrs unique was they **"smiled and smiled with a good heart."**

Living in the Holy Spirit is what separates Jesus from everyone else who had walked on this earth before Him.

The Roman Centurion said:

"Truly this man was the God's Son!"
(Mk 15:39)

What did the Roman centurion see that compelled him make this statement?

Peace radiated from the face of Jesus.

Peace!

In **A Journey with the Holy Spirit** I related what I experienced when I was fired and saw our financial world unraveling.

I started going to daily Mass, and as I walked back from receiving communion, I experienced Peace.

Peace?

Our financial world was unraveling, and for a few brief moments after receiving communion at Mass, I experienced Peace.

Beautiful Peace!

Peace led me to God the Father and is the measure I now use to tell if I am doing His will or mine.

Peace!

In a world filled with stress, our Father offers:

Peace!

What the Centurion also saw in the face of Jesus was:

Joy!

I fell, hit my head and thanked God the Father for the fall and laughed.

Wonderful Joy!

Joy from a hard fall, only God can accomplish this.

Joy!

After I started writing this chapter, I paused and cried. Seventy-five years old and I am just learning how much God the Father Loves me and our family, and I now am starting to realize how much He has taken care of us.

We all know Jesus died as the Lamb of God.

But!

Why don't we know just as strongly that "God took care of Him," and by extension takes care of us?

Jesus Suffers

"*I* **have eagerly desired to eat this Passover with you before I suffer."
(Lk 22: 15)

I said earlier in the book that I have really struggled with the concept of Jesus suffering during His death. I failed to realize what was right in front of me all the time.

In The Agony in the Garden, *in his anguish he prayed more earnestly, and his sweat became like great drops of blood falling down on the ground (Lk 22:44)*

Jesus fully Divine and fully Human: He suffered!

The first blood shed by Jesus was caused by the Holy Spirit pulling slightly away from Jesus, NOT by human hands. Jesus was condemned to death by His testimony NOT the false testimony of the witness. Jesus died when *He bowed his head and gave up his spirit. (Jn 19: 30)*

James Thompson believed that Jesus did not die from exhaus-
tion, the beatings or the 3 hours of crucifixion, but that he
died from agony of mind producing rupture of the heart. His
evidence comes from what happened when the Roman soldier
pierced Christ's left side. The spear released a sudden flow of
blood and water (John 19:34). Not only does this prove that
Jesus was already dead when pierced, but Thompson believes it
is also evidence of cardiac rupture. Respected physiologist
Samuel Houghton believed that only the combination of cruci-
fixion and rupture of the heart could produce this result.
(christiananswers.net)

Jesus fully Devine fully Human: He suffered!

Jesus also suffered from Judas' betrayal, Peter's denial, the remaining disciples abandoning Him, and false testimony of witnesses at His trial.

Jesus fully Devine fully Human: He suffered!

But!

The Lion of God fought back and overcame His suffering and defeated Satan with Outrageous Love!

As I think about this, I now realize Outrageous Love is achieved through suffering.

St. Maximillian Kolbe didn't want to be starved to death. The Martyrs that Seneca spoke of didn't want to be Martyrs.

But!

When the time came to give Glory to God the Father by their death, they did the Father's will.

They suffered a death not of their choosing.

And!

God the Father took care of them, and they defeated Satan through their love of Father, Son and Holy Spirit.

We are all called to be martyrs one way or the other. Many of us are called to be martyrs for the truth of the common good. Then let us resolve every day that we will not give in; that we will suffer, by and with God's grace, whatever he allows for standing up for truth in our speech, and in our actions, whether in public or in private lives; whether in the religious or political/economic spheres. Do you want a better world? It has to start with you and me, here and now. (Catholic News Agency: Martyrdom... What?)

God the Father will take care of us!

How Jesus Died
Applies to Us

Four Life Lessons I Have Learned From the Cross

We are here on earth to learn to do the will of God the Father, for the glory of God the Father.

This is the first and most important lesson.

It's the easiest, and at the same time the hardest.

I lived my younger years doing my will. I was fearful that if I asked God the Father to lead me, what might the Father ask me to do?

Who instilled that fear?

Satan!

At age 70, I finally relented and asked the Father to lead me!

Let me share an example of my doing the will of God the Father since my change in relationship with Him.

All my life I said I would never own a condo.

I don't like rules.

I thought fellow condo owners were unsocial.

I would get lazy because all the yard work was done by professionals.

What would I do with all my free time?

I loved our house.

The facts I didn't want to accept:

I had sore knees and hips from doing the yard work.

We were spending a lot of money on taxes and upkeep.

We didn't have as much time for travel because of the yard work and the extra costs we incurred.

What did God the Father have us do?

You guessed it.

He had us sell our house and buy a condo!

As I faced this decision, I was filled with Joy and Peace. I knew for certain this is what God the Father wanted, and I embraced the change. The Holy Spirit led us to the condo we would buy, and made it possible to sell our house in less than 10 days. This is also how I also knew I was doing God's will. All the pieces fell in place in a very short time span once we found the condo.

I enjoy the condo because:

At the same time we bought the condo, I was also led, by the Holy Spirit, into biking. Gail and I ride 12 miles on the Eastern Trail, which is half a mile from our condo, all the time.

Last year I rode the bike over 1,000 miles.

I discovered Pine Point Beach, which is five miles from the condo where we enjoy walking the beach at low tide, feeling the cool water on our feet with the warm sunshine on our faces.

One day last summer, Gail and I walked four miles on the beach in the morning and that afternoon rode our bikes 12 miles on the Eastern Trail.

Before moving to the condo, I physically couldn't have walked the four miles and ridden my bike an additional 12 miles on the same day.

I also discovered clamming!

My life since we moved into the condo is nothing like I had envisioned it would be.

I now believe God's Outrageous Love was demonstrated to me when we did His will and sold the house and bought the condo.

As I thought back on my life, and as I related in **A Journey with the Holy Spirit**, I told of other times I fought doing the will of God the Father, finally gave in to the Father, and then wished I had done what was being asked of me sooner.

Why?

Joy!

Question: Has God set me up as some sort of playboy because of the condo, with all these fun activities?

Absolutely not!

When I am clamming, walking the beach or biking, I do it in Peace.

No radios!

Cell phone off!

Only the whisper of the Holy Spirit can get to me.

Peace!

Beautiful Peace!

After we moved into the condo, Martha Kelly, a close friend, lent me a copy of **The Seven Story Mountain** by Thomas Merton.

The Seven Story Mountain is Merton's story of finding God by becoming a Trappist monk.

I should note that I tried reading this book when I was in my fifties and couldn't. I feel now that God didn't want me to read it then. I needed to read it now.

Why?

Merton said it was the Peace he experienced at the Trappist monastery, working inside cleaning and outside in the gardens in silence, that drew him into a monastic life.

Peace!

I realized that the quiet time I receive from all the activities associated with our condo was time I could use being with and enjoying the Peace of the Holy Spirit.

Peace was the hook God used in 1980 when I started going to daily Mass.

Merton's book reinforced in me the importance God places on our quiet time together. This is time I can use to grow in our relationship.

A second benefit in buying the condo is that while I am riding the bike, walking the beach or hunting for clams, I have the opportunity to preach the Gospel to people I might meet along the way.

Let me explain.

The Holy Spirit reminded me of a story I had read and saved 20-plus years ago about St. Frances walking toward a town with a fellow friar.

Just before they enter, Frances turns to his companion and tells him he plans on preaching the Gospel there. As they walk through, Frances laughs and plays with the children, comforts someone ill beside the road, and prays with an elderly man who has just lost his wife. As they are leaving, Frances' companion looks at him and says, "I thought we were going to preach the gospel." Frances turns to him and said, "I just did!"

I now preach the Gospel by trying to positively interact with everyone I meet. It amazes me how many people I have met since we moved.

I am also convinced that my actions, walking the walk, speak much louder than my words.

I am now trying to emulate the Lion of God on the Cross!

Life in the Holy Spirit is good!

No, I take that back. It's fantastic!

When I was younger living in the "world," not living in the Spirit, I wanted to become:

Rich
Famous
A Naval Officer
Part of top management at a large company

The above thoughts were not God's. They were mine. And when they crashed and burned, it took a toll out of me.

Why did I have to be so stubborn?

I was not listening for the whisper of the Holy Spirit. I was not trying to grow in the Fruit of the Holy Spirit. I was not trying to do the will of the Father.

My life was I, I, I.

As with the crucified criminal to the right of Jesus, I slowly over the years realized my mistakes, said I was sorry, and asked to be led by the Holy Spirit.

Life is soooooooooooooooo much better.

The second life lesson I learned from the Cross:

Act as Jesus would act when people need help.

Veronica: The definition of her name is True Image.

The Sixth Station of the Cross: *Veronica wipes the face of Jesus.*

"When the Son of Man comes in his glory, and all the angels with him, then he will sit on the throne of his glory. All the nations will be gathered before him, and he will separate people one from another as a shepherd separates the sheep from the goats, and he will put the sheep at his right hand and the goats at the left. Then the king will say to those at his right hand, 'Come, you that are blessed by my Father, inherit the kingdom prepared for you from the foundation of the world;

for I was hungry and you gave me food, I was thirsty and you gave me something to drink, I was a stranger and you welcomed me, I was naked and you gave me clothing, I was sick and you took care of me, I was in prison and you visited me.' **Then the righteous will answer him, 'Lord, when was it that we saw you hungry and gave you food, or thirsty and gave you something to drink? And when was it that we saw you a stranger and welcomed you, or naked and gave you clothing? And when was it that we saw you sick or in prison and visited you?' And the king will answer them, 'Truly I tell you, just as you did it to one of the least of these who are members of my family, you did it to me.' "**
(Emphasis mine Mt 25:31-40)

Side note: I just realized as I was typing the above: sheep on His right—the criminal who asked to be forgiven, and goats on His left—the criminal who said save Yourself and us too.

I mention this because the Bible continues to open up to me, which never ceases to amaze me.

We are the heart, hands, feet and voice of Jesus.

With our heart, hands, feet and voice we have the privilege to speak and act for Jesus here on earth.

When we help someone, we are acting as Jesus helping Jesus.

I would like to share three stories involving our family.

We as a family are not unique!

In each story, neither my sons nor their families, nor I at the time, realized that they were imitating Veronica, imitating Jesus.

Two Christmases ago, Gail and I went to Mississippi to celebrate Christmas with Michael, our eldest son, and his wife Cindy.

At the airport, Mike invited us to go shopping for a family in need. He had met the family as part of his outreach program with the Saint Vincent de Paul Society.

The mother had told Mike there was nothing she could do for her four children for Christmas. She asked Mike if the Saint Vincent de Paul Society would help.

Mike didn't say it, but the Saint Vincent de Paul Society isn't set up for this type of request.

Mike said he knew a few people he could approach, and he would see what they could do.

Mike asked Lee (not her real name) if she had a list of what she wanted to give her kids. She did, and it included two bikes, a game set and other high-priced gifts.

I know Satan whispered to Mike, "She's a loser. Don't waste your money. She's single and has four kids, probably doesn't even know who the dad is. Get her some small trinket, wish them Merry Christmas, and that will be good enough."

The Holy Spirit whispered to Mike, "Get her what she wants."

Mike listened to the Holy Spirit, and we all wrapped the gifts as though these kids were our own.

Lee was a half an hour late to meet us because she missed her bus from work. When she finally arrived, I looked at her and saw Jesus! Lee had been beaten up by bad decisions she had made, but was someone who was also trying to change her life.

I'm sure she had prayed to God for gifts for all her children. I also feel she had faith that her prayer would be answered, because Mike told her if she paid the rent He would take care of the gifts.

What else could she do?

I wish I could say that I realized that night what was happening, but sadly I couldn't.

A few days later, Mike asked me to give a short talk to the St. Vincent de Paul Society. As I have always done, I turned it over to the Holy Spirit to give me the words.

When we arrived at the meeting, my mind was blank. A blank mind for an "A" type personality, who in a few short minutes will be asked to give a 20-minute talk, is scary, especially when I'm talking to people who know and respect Mike.

The Holy Spirit had me tell the story of Lee, and then the Holy Spirit tied Veronica's wiping the face of Jesus into the story of Lee.

Fascinating, I thought, as I was giving the talk. This is where letting the Holy Spirit takeover is fascinating, I am speaking and also analyzing what I am saying, at the same time I am speaking, and learning from what I am saying.

Mike and his family were imitating Veronica, who had imitated Jesus.

The Holy Spirit also had me relate that Lee, the person they were helping, was Jesus.

"Rabbouni;" teaching us how we are to interact with our neighbor and why we are doing this.

We are helping Jesus!

As it always is with God, the story did not end with the giving of the gifts to Lee.

Lee told Jamie, Mike's wife's son, who was with Mike at her apartment, that she worked at the local hospital in Jackson.

Jamie told Lee that his grandfather had been in the hospital for three days, and was not doing well.

Lee said she would stop in and see him.

Lee bought a card and a cross, from her need, and gave it to Jamie's grandfather.

Jamie's grandfather was Jesus, Lee was Veronica imitating Jesus, and amazingly, Jamie's grandfather left the hospital the next day.

Beautiful, isn't it?

"God will take care of Him," and He took care of Lee's children and Jamie's grandfather.

The second story:

David, our middle son, and his wife Sonia decided they wanted to adopt a child.

The process took almost two years, and at times was very frustrating for both David and Sonia. Finally they were told that a 7-year-old Ethiopian boy named Gediyon could be their new son.

Dave and Sonia flew to Ethiopia, met and fell in love at once with Gediyon.

Many of us questioned how their children Brenna and Andre would interact with Gediyon.

Well, Gediyon arrived at their home and was greeted with 100 percent acceptance.

Gail and I were amazed how quickly Gediyon was fully assimilated into their family.

It's like he has always been there.

Gediyon is Jesus, an orphan. Dave and his family are Veronica, imitating Jesus.

I don't have to say this, but I will: Gediyon is a blessing for our entire family.

"God will take care of Him," and found Gediyon a loving home, and we gained another grandchild.

The third story:

John, our youngest son, and Heather, his wife, heard of a local family in need. They talked with their daughters Hannah and Kendall about how they could be involved.

The family in need was Jesus, and John and his family were Veronica imitating Jesus.

Jesus said when you give; don't let the left hand know what the right hand is doing. (Mt 6:3)

This is exactly what John's family did.

They went to a dinner being held by the local community to help the family, left a plain envelope, wished all a Merry Christmas and walked out filled with Joy.

"God will take care of Him," and the family was Jesus being helped by the outpouring of John's family and many of the other families in the Portland community.

I have repeated *"God will take care of Him"* because it is so obvious when you see God working in our lives that you have to ask yourself, as I now am: Why didn't I see this earlier?

These are everyday people who reached out and helped their neighbors.

At age 74, in Mississippi, I realized that the person being helped is Jesus, and the person helping is also Jesus.

Yes, Jesus. He spent his life curing the sick, feeding the hungry and raising the dead. Now we have the privilege to carry on His work.

We are His heart, hands, feet and voice.

Beautiful, isn't it?

I remember an expression that is used in government service, when a person is asked by the President of the United States to do a particular job for our country. The expression is: "Serving at the pleasure of the President."

How much more is this true for our doing the will of God the Father, and serving those He brings into our lives?

Yes, He brings them into our lives.

The above three stories are not about good luck. They are stories of people accepting a challenge placed before them by God.

I am sure our sons and their families, and I, for that matter, didn't realize then that what they were doing was helping Jesus by imitating Jesus.

I do know they were all filled with Joy!

Think of all the good that takes place every day.

A small fraction makes the news which is sad.

The third life lesson I learned from the Cross:

Forgive those who transgress against us.

Below is a news story of an Amish community's reaction to a school shooting when five of their children were killed:

On October 2, 2006, a shooting occurred at the West Nickel Mines School, an Amish one-room schoolhouse in the Old Order Amish community of Nickel Mines, a village in Bart Township of Lancaster County, Pennsylvania. Gunman Charles Carl Roberts IV took hostages and shot 10 girls (aged 6–13), killing five, before committing suicide in the schoolhouse. The emphasis on forgiveness and reconciliation in the response of the Amish community was widely discussed in the national media. The West Nickel Mines School was torn down, and a new one-room schoolhouse, the New Hope School, was built at another location.

On the day of the shooting, a grandfather of one of the murdered Amish girls was heard warning some young relatives not to hate the killer, saying, **"We must not think evil of this man."** *Another Amish father noted,* **"He had a mother and a wife and a soul and now he's standing before a just God."** *Jack Meyer, a member of the Brethren community living near the Amish in Lancaster County, explained:* **"I don't think there's anybody here that wants to do anything but forgive and not only reach out to those who have suffered a loss in that way but to reach out to the family of the man who committed these acts."**

A Roberts family spokesman said an Amish neighbor comforted the Roberts family hours after the shooting and extended forgiveness to them. **Amish community members visited and comforted Roberts' widow, parents and parents-in-law. One Amish man held Roberts' sobbing father in his arms, reportedly for as long as an hour, to comfort him. The Amish have also set up a charitable fund for the family of the shooter. About 30 members of the Amish community attended Roberts' funeral, and Marie Roberts, the widow of the killer, was one of the** *few outsiders invited to the funeral of one of the victims.*

Marie Roberts wrote an open letter to her Amish neighbors thanking them for their forgiveness, grace, and mercy. She wrote, "Your love for our family has helped to provide the healing we so desperately need. Gifts you've given have touched our hearts in a way no words can describe. Your compassion has reached beyond our family, beyond our community, and is changing our world, and for this we sincerely thank you." The Amish do not normally accept charity, but due to the extreme nature of the tragedy, donations were accepted. Richie Lauer, director of the Anabaptist Foundation, said the Amish community, whose religious beliefs prohibit them from having health insurance will likely use the donations to help pay the medical costs of the hospitalized children.

*Some commentators criticized the quick and complete forgiveness with which the Amish responded, arguing that forgiveness is inappropriate when no remorse has been expressed, and that such an attitude runs the risk of denying the existence of evil, while others were supportive. Donald Kraybill and two other scholars of Amish life noted that "letting go of grudges" is a deeply rooted value in Amish culture, which remembers forgiving martyrs including Dirk Willems and Jesus himself. **They explained that the Amish willingness to forgo vengeance does not undo the tragedy or pardon the wrong, but rather constitutes a first step toward a future that is more hopeful.***
(Emphasis mine, Wikipedia)

The Amish imitated Jesus on the Cross. They learned from "Rabbouni," and when events forced them to practice what they learned, they acted in a way that stunned many in the "world."

I have shared this story in the hope that as you watch current events unfold, you will ask yourself the question:

"How would I react?"

Sadly, I have reacted by wanting to seek revenge.

Satan!

Do outside events control you or are you a reflection of Jesus?

Are you reflecting Love, Joy and Peace in everything that happens in your life?

Are you thanking God the Father for all the difficulties He allows in your life?

This is what being a Christian means. At first it doesn't sound possible.

Satan tells us constantly that doing the Father's will is impossible.

When Satan tells us not to listen to God the Father, tell Satan to get behind you!

Live in the Holy Spirit!

Experience a lifestyle better than anything you have ever experienced before, because God is a God of Outrageous Love here and now!

Jesus needed the Cross to prove to a skeptical world that doing the will of God the Father and living in the Holy Spirit is the life we are all called to live.

The fourth life lesson I learned from the Cross:

Thank God the Father for the difficulties He allows in your life.

In our first book, **A Journey with the Holy Spirit**, one of the chapters was titled "Thank you, Father!"

When I read **Prison to Praise** by Merlin Carothers, it changed my life.

Merlin, a Methodist minister, said we are to thank God the Father for all the difficulties that He, God the Father, **allows** to come into our life.

Since I started praying these simple words:

"Thank you, Father, for the difficulty of ...."my life has changed to the positive, so much so that I can't believe it.

A quick recap of what God told Merlin:

Merlin related in **Prison to Praise** that one day God spoke to him.

God asked Merlin, "Do you thank Me for the death of My Son?" Merlin said yes.

I sadly said no. I didn't say those specific words.

I do now!

Next, God asked Merlin, "Do you thank Me for the nails driven into His hands?"

Merlin said yes. I said no.

Lastly, God asked Merlin, "Do you thank Me for the nail driven into His feet?"

Merlin said yes. I said no.

How could I be so stupid?

How could I be so careless?

God then told Merlin, "If you thank Me for the death of My Son, the Nails driven into His hands and feet, then I want you, Merlin, to thank Me for the difficulties I **allow** in your life."

Wow. I was bowled over.

This, to me, explained everything!

Jesus had a life filled with difficulties.

Go back to the New Testament section of this book.

They tried to throw Him over a cliff.

They were always trying to trap Him.

I would call these difficulties, wouldn't you?

If God the Father allowed these difficulties, and many more, to happen to Jesus, shouldn't we expect the same?

In fact, as I type this, wouldn't I feel left out if I didn't have any difficulties?

Remember:

Suffering is only to be thought a positive experience in the case of achieving a higher meaning of life, such as Jesus suffering for the lives of other Christians. Suffering is the time to find God and value faith while doing so. This allows Christians to face the reality of human experience with suffering and find an understanding in the divine.
(Wikipedia)

In Merlin's second book, **Power of Praise**, he tells of many healings, broken marriages reconciled, major illnesses cured, alcohol and drug abuse healed, all turned around by the power of this prayer.

A year later, a good friend, Charlie Pinette, who gave me **Prison to Praise,** gave me a pamphlet titled "**Here Animal,**" also written by Merlin Carothers.

This opened my eyes further about the power of thanking God the Father for the difficulties He **allows** in our life, and the relationship God the Father longs to have with us.

A summary of what Merlin wrote in **Here Animal:**

No prison system likes a prisoner who attacks their guards.

"The Animal" hated everyone.

This prison had a concrete cell 16 feet deep that was 8x8 with a small steel door at the top.

"The hole"!

State law allowed that a prisoner could spend only seven days in the hole.

After seven days, most prisoners came out changed.

"The Animal" went down for his first stay of seven days, came out and within 24 hours slugged a guard.

He went back into the hole.

After weeks and months of repeated trips to the hole, the man was called "The Animal" by the guards for his behavior.

One day, months after this had all started, a guard read **Prison to Praise** and felt if anyone needed this book it was "The Animal."

He hated "The Animal" so much that he kicked the book between the grates in the trap door and said, "Read this, Animal."

Alone with nothing to do, the prisoner read **Prison to Praise** by the faint light that came through the steel bars 16 feet above him.

"The Animal" mocked everything Merlin had written. He scoffed at the idea of thanking God for things that had happened to him.

*In **derision and scorn** he said, "Okay, God, I thank you for that three-foot cement wall ... see, it's still there. Thanking you didn't do anything."*

Laughing and mocking, *"The Animal" thanked God for the damp coldness, the numerous cockroaches, his hunger pains and aching bones.*

Exhausting his thanks for what he could see, he thanked God for the guards he hated, the prisoners who despised him, the judge who sentenced him, his worthless attorney, the witnesses who lied about him, the policeman who arrested him, the people who kicked and beat him when he was a boy, and for his drunken, abusive parents.

When "The Animal" finished his list, he went back and started all over. Hour after hour he repeated this prayer. He laughed and dared God to do something.

Anything!

On the seventh day, the ladder was lowered and "The Animal" crawled out.

The guard was flabbergasted.

"The Animal" was smiling.

His eyes looked happy.

He was a different man.

Something had happened.
(Emphasis mine, Here Animal)

"The Animal" later explained to Merlin that a man appeared to him in his cell and said three words:

"I LOVE YOU."

Eventually the prisoner was released, pardoned by the governor, and is now a prison chaplain.

What a story!

What jumped out at me?

His prayer: Laughing and mocking God is a form of prayer?

Prayer, for me, has always been: God the Father is up there, and I'm down here. I'm not going to let my true feelings come out for fear I would upset God the Father.

How stupid of me!

God is called Father because He wants a relationship with us.

The relationship God the Father wants is a relationship that is not at arm's length, but is up front and personal.

We are called sons and daughters (2 Co 6:18). Therefore we are asked to get into a full relationship with the Father, and if that means getting in His face, that's okay.

God can take it!

I smile every time I pray the words "Thank you, Father, for the difficulty of.........." If I don't smile at first, I keep repeating the prayer, like "The Animal," until I do smile.

My smile tells me I am linked to the Holy Spirit because Satan can't smile.

Being in an honest relationship with God and thanking God for my difficulties and blessings works!

Why?

The press tells us that many people today suffer from stress.

I believe it!

God sees me, a sinner, trying to grow in the Fruit of the Holy Spirit, thanking Him for all the difficulties He has **allowed** in my life, and thanking Him for the blessings that He has poured out into our lives.

And God sees someone else complaining about everything going on in their life.

Who would you or God rather listen to—the complainers or the persons filled with Joy and Praise?

I'm not a theologian, but I do know the answer, and so do you.

In Exodus we see the reaction of God to the constant complaining of the Jews. At one point God threatened to wipe them all out, and Moses had to beg God to relent. (Ex 32:10)

I thanked God for my sore knees. The Holy Spirit brought to mind an exercise I should do, and they were healed because of my doing the exercise.

Yesterday, I thanked God six months after having malware infect our computer, which a computer neighbor friend of mine and I couldn't root out.

Don Hale, a close high school friend who I hadn't talked to in months, called and I told Him of my malware problem. He led me to a web page that solved the problem. He called me a day after I thanked God the Father for the difficulty of the malware in the computer.

Why did I wait six months to thank God for the difficulty of the malware, you might ask?

I'm a slow learner!

I have also learned that by my thanking God the Father for my difficulties, when they are resolved, as the above examples illustrate, I am given the chance to offer Praise to God, as I have just done, on a very personal basis. The healing of the knees and the getting rid of the malware are just two examples.

There are many, many, many more!

The really good news is that Don and I revitalized our friendship.

I am telling the story about the computer problem because this would be one of the last things I would consider praying about.

I waited six months!

That's not a relationship!

In a true relationship everything is on the table, nothing is held back.

Why?

Joy!

Knowing God is always with me, as He was with Jesus on the Cross, fills me with Joy and Peace.

I'm not a second-class citizen.

Jesus said I am His brother! (Lk 8:21)

We are so special that God the Father sent his Son, Jesus, to climb up on the Cross, so we could learn of God's Outrageous Love.

Always Give God Praise and Thanksgiving

I was lying in bed the other night when I realized, Holy Spirit, the most important chapter hadn't been written.

We are told in the Bible to offer Praise and Thanksgiving to God all the time. (Heb 13:15)

Why?

Jesus dying on the Cross, so all men might be justified.

That is an excellent reason and should be the only reason, but this sadly didn't completely answer my question.

Gail and I are celebrating 50 years of marriage this year.

I can't believe how fast the time has flown by!

I thank God every day for bringing Gail into my life.

Every day, at supper, I thank God for Gail, her wonderful meals, and this day we have lived together.

I realized I have a choice.

Shower her with praise and thanksgiving.

Or:

Don't say anything.

Or:

Tell her the meals suck and she should take some cooking lessons.

Of the above three choices, which one will lead to 50 years of a joyful marriage?

Wouldn't God be the same way?

We should thank God and Praise Him for the difficulties He has **allowed** in our lives, and in doing so have Faith that God will take care of us.

And God does!

This may seem hard to believe, but my experience is that some difficulties are resolved quickly, and some take time.

Have faith!

Don't quit thanking Him!

And

Don't stop thanking Him until you smile!

I said all this earlier.

What I didn't say was:

Why?

When the difficulty is resolved, you will feel Joy!

God is taking care of you!

Once you Praise God for the difficulties in your life, you will also want to thank Him for all the Blessings He has showered on you.

Giving Thanks and Praise now becomes very easy!

Or:

You can ignore God and take credit for all you have done on your own.

Indifference!

Or:

You can hate God!

Of the above three scenarios, which will help you grow in a life of Love, Joy and Peace?

I'm not a Theologian and probably you aren't either, but you know the answer!

One last question has to be answered.

Why do we have to praise God at all times?

The answer, I finally realized, is easy.

At first I felt God needed our praise. Satan put this thought in my mind.

That can't be true because it makes God less than God.

God is the Creator!

The Earth is His footstool. (Act 7:49)

The reason God asks us to praise Him all the time is to block out Satan!

If we are Praising God for what we have...
we can't be envious of what others have!

If we are Praising God for what we are doing...
we can't be filled with doubt about the future! We are living in the present with I AM!

If we are Praising God about our financial well-being no matter what that is...
we can't be stressed about our financial matters!

God will take care of us, as He already has. Why would He stop now?

It's easy. Imitate Jesus, God's Lion, and live in the "Spirit World" doing the will of the Father.

Jesus said, "If you had faith the size of a mustard seed, you could say to this mulberry tree, 'Be uprooted and planted in the sea,' and it would obey you."
(Lk 17:6)

Over the years I have heard people say Jesus was kidding when He said this, or they said He was using this as an example.

I don't believe them!

Look at the miracles Jesus preformed: Raising the dead, feeding 5,000 people, curing the sick, just to mention three.

No, Jesus meant what He said about the mulberry bush.

For a long time I have realized my faith was much smaller than a mustard seed.

The question I asked myself, and couldn't answer until I worked on this book, was: How do I grow in my Faith in God?

At first I wrote that growing in Faith is a five-step process.

The Holy Spirit reminded me we are all different and with God there is no such thing as the same five steps for all people.

I reflected again on my life and realized:

I started praying for an increase in the Fruit of the Holy Spirit. As I grew in the Fruit of the Holy Spirit, I realized I was living as Jesus lived, in Love, Joy and Peace.

I embraced my new lifestyle.

Decades afterward, on one November night in 2010, I realized, Holy Spirit, I had to let go and let God the Father lead me through the whisper of the Holy Spirit.

God is first, I'm second!

I wrote of my experiences of living in the Fruit of the Holy Spirit, and letting God lead me, in **A Journey with the Holy Spirit**.

All I will say now is I wish I had done this much sooner.

Four years ago, when I read **Prison to Praise**, my life took another dramatic turn.

I started praying, "Thank you, Father, for the difficulties you have **allowed** to come into my life."

I realized I was, and am, building a relationship with God, and I embrace that relationship.

I still didn't have the answer on how to grow in my Faith in God, though.

This year, as I worked on this book, I realized that if I asked God to take care of me, He will.

This prayer is powerful!

Over the course of the book, I wrote that I couldn't figure out, at first, how God took care of Jesus, on the Cross.

As I started writing the chapter "God Will Take Care of Him," the bells went off, and the puzzle, for me, about how I grow in Faith was answered.

"God will take care of Him" is a very powerful prayer, because it shifts total control of my life to God.

Shifting control to God because of past encounters with God taking care of me increases my Faith that God will take care of me now and in the future.

Maybe you haven't had any past encounters with God taking care of you.

Start now!

If you have a difficulty, and most of the time we do, thank God now for the difficulty, and thank Him until you smile, and then pray, that you know God will take care of you.

I know this sounds strange.

But start!

Take that leap of Faith, and try asking God to take care of you.

When God does take care of you, and He will, then it is easy to offer praise and thanksgiving.

Notice I am not telling God how he will take care of me only praying and knowing He will.

God takes care of us, just as any loving dad or mother would do for their son or daughter.

Question: If you go to a doctor and he heals you, don't you thank him? Wouldn't you tell others about what the doctor did, so that they may take advantage of his skill?

Why would God be different?

This chapter started out asking why Praising God at all times should be an important part of our lives.

The answer is, because God the Father takes care of us, all the time.

The fact that we haven't acknowledged His taking care of us doesn't mean it hasn't happened.

I went for many years, actually way too many years, without thanking God for all He has done for me, and our family.

I've changed, and I love the new person I am becoming.

I started sharing my experiences with the men at the Cumberland County Jail, and gave them a handout, so they could try these prayers.

Growing in Faith:

Learn and grow in the Fruit of The Holy Spirit: **Love, Joy, and Peace,** by praying for an increase in **Patience, Kindness, Generosity, Faithfulness, Gentleness, and Self-**

Control.
(Galatians Chapter 5:23)

Thank God the Father for the difficulties He has allowed in your life by praying: **"Thank you Father** *for the difficulty of............"* *After that, pray:* **I know God will take care of me,** *and when God does take care of you,* **thank Him!**

In two short weeks after starting this process, three men announced that their sentences had been changed.

They were on top of the world.

The first to respond said his sentence was reduced from eight years to three years.

The second man said his wife wanted to divorce him and take the kids. He could only keep the kids if he got out of jail in eight months or less.

Earlier he was told he would have to serve a three year term.

He thanked God for the difficulty of the three-year sentence, and next said, "I know you will take care of me." And when I saw him two weeks later, he said his sentence was reduced to eight months.

He was on top of the world!

The third to respond said he wanted to do time served and be let out.

He was given a three-year sentence. One of the other men mocked him and said, "God didn't take care of you."

The prayer didn't work!

He replied that if he was given time served, he would have been deported.

When they gave him the three-year sentence, they told him he could stay in the country.

One note about this person: He has always claimed he was innocent. I for one believe him. I have had this thought only twice in twenty years of the prison ministry. I also believe he will get out before the three years are up because he is so positive, and like "The Animal," his life has changed.

He changed and embraces the change.

A fourth man said he couldn't raise his arm above his head. I told him to thank God for the difficulty of not being able to raise his arm above his head, and know God will take care of him.

Next week he didn't say a thing.

He didn't have to.

He raised his arm above his head.

They asked God the Father to take care of them, and He did!

We all celebrated, but I also reminded them their battle with Satan never stops.

I have put a copy of this prayer in the back of the book. Hopefully you will tear the out the page, learn the prayers and put them into action.

I am saddened by the men who won't try to change their life. I guess they think if they continue doing the same thing, life will somehow change.

Isn't this type of thinking the same as rearranging the deck chairs on the Titanic?

I can't condemn them, because in my younger years I would have reacted exactly the same way.

Sadly, I knew it all.

Last Thoughts

No other Prophet (Moses or Mohamed, to mention two) or any Greek or Roman god submitted themselves to death— and more importantly, death on a cross.

Jesus talked the talk, and because of His Cross, walked the walk.

In the movie **The Passion of the Christ**, director Mel Gibson ends the movie with a giant tear coming down from heaven and crashing onto the earth, causing an earthquake.

At first I thought the tear was symbolic of God the Father crying for what Jesus had gone through for our salvation.

I now feel this is entirely wrong!

The tear is from God the Father, but the tear is for all who still refuse to accept a God of Outrageous Love and live in the "Spirit World."

Jesus the Lion of God defeated Satan!

We are justified!

By his death on the Cross, Jesus taught us how to live our lives.

How to fight Satan!

When we fail to follow Jesus' teaching from the Cross, Heaven on earth is replaced with stress, drug and alcohol addictions, hatred, envy and the like.

Nothing in life is really new.

God told Adam and Eve not to eat the fruit from the apple tree.

They ate the apple, and were thrown out of the Garden of Eden.

Two thousand years before Jesus, Moses told the Jews before they crossed into the Promised Land that they had to choose between life and prosperity, and death and adversity.

See, I have set before you today life and prosperity, death and adversity. If you obey the commandments of the Lord your God that I am commanding you today, by loving the Lord your God, walking in his ways, and observing his commandments, decrees, and ordinances, then you shall live and become numerous, and the Lord your God will bless you in the land that you are entering to possess. But if your heart turns away and you do not hear, but are led astray to bow down to other gods and serve them, I declare to you today that you shall perish; you shall not live long in the land that you are crossing the Jordan to enter and possess. I call heaven and earth to witness against you today that I have set before you life and death, blessings and curses. Choose life so that you and your descendants may live, loving the Lord your God, obeying him, and holding fast to him; for that means life to you and length of days, so that you may live in

the land that the Lord swore to give to your ances-
tors, to Abraham, to Isaac, and to Jacob.
(Emphasis mine, De 30: 15-20)

As you read the Old Testament, it becomes very clear that the Jewish people chose death and adversity over the two thousand years before the birth of Jesus, by worshiping false gods.

They paid dearly for it.

In Galatians, Paul compares the works of the flesh to the Fruit of the Holy Spirit.

The Works of the Flesh
Now the works of the flesh are obvious: fornication, impurity, licentiousness, idolatry, sorcery, enmities, strife, jealousy, an-ger, quarrels, dissensions, factions, envy, drunkenness, carous-ing, **and things like these***. I am warning you, as I warned you before: those who do such things will not inherit the king-dom of God.*
(Emphasis mine Ga 5:19-21)

Notice, Paul said *"and things like these."* The above list, then, is not complete.

The Fruit of the Spirit
By contrast, the fruit of the Spirit is love, joy, peace, patience, kindness, generosity, faithfulness, gentleness, and self-control. There is no law against such things. And those who belong to Christ Jesus have crucified the flesh with its passions and de-sires. If we live by the Spirit, let us also be guided by the Spir-it.
(Ga 5:22-25)

There are only nine Fruit of the Holy Spirit, no expansion, just nine Fruit, as compared to living in the flesh, which is unlim-ited.

The Jews didn't have the advantage of the Holy Spirit.

Baptized Christians do!

If we choose to live life in the Holy Spirit, Love, Joy and Peace will be our inheritance, just as Moses and St. Paul promised.

I am reminded of a parable about a farmer who found a pearl of great value, and sold everything so he might have it. (Mt 13: 46)

For 74 years I believed the pearl was Jesus, and I was the farmer. The only problem I had with this thought was, I haven't sold everything.

Soooooooooooo:

I have a problem.

Msgr. Henchal, in one of his Sunday homilies said, "Consider a different interpretation of this Parable. You are the pearl and Jesus the farmer."

I was blown away.

He's right!

Why?

The Cross!

At the request of His Father, and living fully in the Holy Spirit, Jesus gave everything, blood and water. He emptied Himself fully so that we might be justified!

We are that special to God!

We win!

I was reminded, Holy Spirit, that when Christopher Columbus landed in the New World, he stepped off the boat that brought him to shore and planted the Spanish flag in the ground and claimed the land for the King and Queen of Spain.

When Jesus died on the Cross, He was taken down from the Cross, but the Cross remained standing.

Today, all around the world, the Cross continues to remain standing!

The flag of the "Spirit World" waves stronger every day.

Jesus, through His death, established a new world, a life in the Holy Spirit, a "Spirit World," a world filled with Love, Joy and Peace.

How did He do this?

Jesus spoke from His Cross.

He showed Love for His Father—*First Commandment: love the Lord your God with all your heart, and with all soul, with your entire mind*—by doing His the Father's will.

Jesus loved His mother by telling the disciple He loved, while hanging on the Cross, that Mary was his mother (Jn 19:27)— *The Fifth Commandment: Honor thy Father and Mother.*

Jesus Forgave the criminal on His right and welcomed him into Heaven, today. Jesus the Good Shepard found the lost sheep. (Lk 24: 42-43)

He forgave those who crucified Him— *"Father, forgive them; for they do not know what they are doing." (Lk 23: 34)*

He said, "I am thirsty." (Jn 19:28) His thirst is for the Mercy and Justice that would be established because of His death.

He said, "It is finished."(Jn 19: 30) The old "world" is finished, and a new "Spirit World" is established.

The Lion of God defeated Satan by Outrageous Love.

The Lion of God taught us to thank God the Father for the difficulties He, the Father, **allows** in our lives, so that we might establish a close relationship with the Father through the Son in the Holy Spirit because we are His sons and daughters.

The Lion of God won!

My Promise to You

E very day I will pray that you will:

Grow in Faith by:

Learning and growing in the Fruit of The Holy Spirit: *Love, Joy, and Peace,* by praying for an increase in *Patience, Kindness, Generosity, Faithfulness, Gentleness, Self-Control.*
(Galatians Chapter 5:23)

Thank God the Father for the difficulties He has **allowed** in your life by praying: **"Thank you Father for the difficulty of ...."** After that, pray: **I know God will take care of me,** and when God does take care of you: **thank Him!**

And God will take care of me in the writing of this book

H oly Spirit:

You might notice I give full credit to the Holy Spirit on the front cover, and throughout this book. I know my skills, and being an author is not one of them.

A Journey with The Holy Spirit was about my life, and therefore easier, if I may use the word easier, to write.

A Lion Dead to the Lord required extensive use of scripture and outside articles. I was amazed how the Holy Spirit led me to these resources.

I never used an outline. I just sat down and typed His words.

There have been numerous revisions, and each time more has opened up to me.

I had hoped to have the book published over a year and a half ago.

What I'm learning is Patience, and the Joy of working with the Holy Spirit.

I truly look forward to our next book, **I Believe**.

I want to thank my wife, Gail, our family and friends who worked with me on this project.

Knowing my shortcomings as a writer, the Spirit led me to recruit my wife Gail, Charlie Pinette, my brother David, Brian Collins and Marie Aceto to review the first draft for its obvious errors, and there were many.

After countless revisions, I next asked my brother Roger to review the book for readability. He pointed out many other weaknesses. We went back to work and made further changes.

Lastly, I asked our eldest son Mike to review the latest edition. He made further great suggestions, and we had a great time together working on this project.

Through all the above people, God took care of me in writing His book.

I also want to thank Andre, David's and Sonia's youngest son, for asking me, from time to time, when **A Lion Dead to the Lord** would be done.

Here it is, Andre!

Brian Collins

Brian told Mike he was mad that he hadn't been asked to do the cover for **A Journey with the Holy Spirit.**
Brian is a great graphic artist, and I asked Brian if he would do this cover.
Brian said yes!
An interesting thing happened to Brian.
I loved the cover he first designed, but I didn't like the black background. I felt it was too negative.
Brian made some changes, which I loved, and then a few hours later sent me even more changes.
The Holy Spirit was working in Brian's life as he worked on the cover.
I am thrilled with the cover he designed. If you look carefully, the Lion is at Peace.

Tim Nudd

My editor, and personal friend, the person who makes our books look and read truly professional, signed on for our second book.
I recruited Tim the first day we met and am so glad we're working together again on this project.
With a young family, and a demanding job, Tim's time is precious; making me all the more appreciative of the work he has done and is doing on this book.

Susan Conroy

Susan is Maine's most popular spiritual writer.
She has written: **Mother Teresa's Lessons of Love and Secrets of Sanctity, Legacy of Love, The End of the Present World, The Plays of St. Therese' of Lisieux,** and **Coming to Christ.** Susan also has a series on EWTN, **Speaking of Saints,** and is working on a new series for EWTN.
I have read **Mother Teresa's Lessons of Love** and **The End of the Present World,** and enjoyed both.
Susan has given me the advice I needed to keep this project going.
Web: www.susanconroy.com

Ted Butler

God brings people into our lives, and the moment you meet them, you know they will be lifelong friends.
Ted and Mila, Ted's wife, are two of these people.
Because Ted writes a very interesting article twice a week about silver, I asked Ted to review **A Lion Dead to the Lord.**
I thank Ted for his very kind words.
Ted's web page: www.butlerresearch.com

I would like to thank **Msgr. Henchal, Msgr. Paul Stefanko, Rev. Innocent Okozi, Fr. John Knox and all the Priests and religious God has brought into my life.**
It is because of them I learned of God's Outrageous Love.
Many of these people never knew they were an important part of my journey in finding God by what they said and did.

Foundation for Praise – Merlin Carothers

Merlin took the hallelujah train home to Jesus on 11/11/2013. I want to thank the Foundation of Praise for giving me permission to use parts of the pamphlet "Here Animal." Prison to Praise changed my life!

The Foundation for Praise sells Prison to Praise, Power in Praise, Amazing Power of Faith, and "Here Animal."

Web page: www.foundationofpraise.org

Phone: 760-741-2755

93309436R00107

Made in the USA
Columbia, SC
09 April 2018